W9-BCV-133

HUMBER LIBRARIES LAKESHORE CAMPUS
3199 Lakeshore Blvd West
TORONTO, ON.   M8V 1K8

DISCARD

How Journalism Uses History

How Journalism Uses History examines the various ways in which journalism uses history and historical sources in order to better understand the relationships between journalists, historians and journalism scholars. It highlights the ambiguous overlap between the role of the historian and that of the journalist, and underlines that there no longer seems to be reason to accept that one begins only where the other ends.

With Journalism Studies as a developing subject area throughout the world, journalism history is becoming a particularly vivacious field. As such, *How Journalism Uses History* argues that, if historical study of this kind is to achieve its full potential, there needs to be a fuller and more consistent engagement with other academics studying the past: political, social and cultural historians in particular, but also scholars working in politics, sociology, literature and linguistics.

Contributors in this book discuss the core themes which inform history's relationship with journalism from a wide range of geographical and methodological perspectives. They aim to create more ambitious conversations about using journalism both as a source for under-standing the past, and for clarifying ideas about its role as constituent of the public sphere in using discourse and tradition to connect contemporary audiences with history.

This book was originally published as a special issue of *Journalism Practice*.

Martin Conboy is Professor of Journalism History at the University of Sheffield, UK. He is also co-director of the Centre for the Study of Journalism and History based in Sheffield. Research interests include the representation of national identity, popular journalism and celebrity culture. He is the author of six books on the language and history of journalism and is on the editorial boards of *Journalism Studies*, *Media History*, *Journalism: Theory, Practice and Criticism* and *Memory Studies*. He is also co-editor of the book series *Journalism Studies: Key Texts*.

Journalism Studies: Theory and Practice

Series editor: Bob Franklin, Cardiff School of Journalism, Media and Cultural Studies, UK

The journal *Journalism Studies* was established at the turn of the new millennium by Bob Franklin. It was launched in the context of a burgeoning interest in the scholarly study of journalism and an expansive global community of journalism scholars and researchers. The ambition was to provide a forum for the critical discussion and study of journalism as a subject of intellectual inquiry but also an arena of professional practice. Previously, the study of journalism in the UK and much of Europe was a fairly marginal branch of the larger disciplines of media, communication and cultural studies; only a handful of Universities offered degree programmes in the subject. *Journalism Studies* has flourished and succeeded in providing the intended public space for discussion of research on key issues within the field, to the point where in 2007 a sister journal, *Journalism Practice,* was launched to enable an enhanced focus on practice-based issues, as well as foregrounding studies of journalism education, training and professional concerns. Both journals are among the leading ranked journals within the field and publish six issues annually, in electronic and print formats. From the outset, the publication of themed issues has been a commitment for both journals. Their purpose is first, to focus on highly significant or neglected areas of the field; second, to facilitate discussion and analysis of important and topical policy issues; and third, to offer readers an especially high quality and closely focused set of essays, analyses and discussions.

The *Journalism Studies: Theory and Practice* book series draws on a wide range of these themed issues from both journals and thereby extends the critical and public forum provided by them. The Editor of the journals works closely with guest editors to ensure that the books achieve relevance for readers and the highest standards of research rigour and academic excellence. The series makes a significant contribution to the field of journalism studies by inviting distinguished scholars, academics and journalism practitioners to discuss and debate the central concerns within the field. It also reaches a wider readership of scholars, students and practitioners across the social sciences, humanities and communication arts, encouraging them to engage critically with, but also to interrogate, the specialist scholarly studies of journalism which this series provides.

Previously published titles:

Mapping the Magazine
Comparative Studies in Magazine
   Journalism
Edited by Tim Holmes

The Future of Newspapers
Edited by Bob Franklin

Language and Journalism
Edited by John E. Richardson

The Future of Journalism
Edited by Bob Franklin

New and forthcoming for 2012:

Exploration in Global Media Ethics
*Edited by Muhammad Ayish and
   Shakuntala Rao*

Foreign Correspondence
*Edited by John Maxwell Hamilton and
   Regina G. Lawrence*

How Journalism Uses History
Edited by Martin Conboy

Lifestyle Journalism
Edited by Folker Hanusch

How Journalism Uses History

Edited by
Martin Conboy

Routledge
Taylor & Francis Group

LONDON AND NEW YORK

HUMBER LIBRARIES LAKESHORE CAMPUS
3199 Lakeshore Blvd West
TORONTO, ON. M8V 1K8

DISCARD

First published 2012
by Routledge
2 Park Square, Milton Park, Abingdon, Oxon, OX14 4RN

Simultaneously published in the USA and Canada
by Routledge
711 Third Avenue, New York, NY 10017

Routledge is an imprint of the Taylor & Francis Group, an informa business

© 2012 Taylor & Francis

This book is a reproduction of *Journalism Practice*, volume 5, issue 5. The Publisher requests to those authors who may be citing this book to state, also, the bibliographical details of the special issue on which the book was based.

All rights reserved. No part of this book may be reprinted or reproduced or utilised in any form or by any electronic, mechanical, or other means, now known or hereafter invented, including photocopying and recording, or in any information storage or retrieval system, without permission in writing from the publishers.

Trademark notice: Product or corporate names may be trademarks or registered trademarks, and are used only for identification and explanation without intent to infringe.

British Library Cataloguing in Publication Data
A catalogue record for this book is available from the British Library

ISBN 13: 978-0-415-62290-5

Typeset in Helvetica
by Taylor & Francis Books

Publisher's Note
The publisher would like to make readers aware that the chapters in this book may be referred to as articles as they are identical to the articles published in the special issue. The publisher accepts responsibility for any inconsistencies that may have arisen in the course of preparing this volume for print.

Printed and bound in the United States of America by Publishers Graphics, LLC on sustainably sourced paper.

Contents

NOTES ON CONTRIBUTORS

Andrés Cañizález, PhD, is a Professor of Journalism at the Universidad Católica Andrés Bello in Venezuela, where he is also the co-ordinator of the programme of Freedom of Expression. He has published over a dozen books and many articles regarding journalism and media in Latin America. In 2010 he was awarded the international "Titus Brandsma Award" for his outstanding academic contributions and commitment to freedom of expression in Latin America.

Martin Conboy is Professor of Journalism History at the University of Sheffield. He is also the co-director of the Centre for the Study of Journalism and History based in Sheffield. His research interests include the representation of national identity, popular journalism and celebrity culture. He is the author of six books on the language and history of journalism and is on the editorial boards of *Journalism Studies, Media History, Journalism: Theory, Practice and Criticism* and *Memory Studies*. He is also co-editor of the book series *Journalism Studies: Key Texts*.

Christopher B. Daly, a former journalist, is an Associate Professor of Journalism at Boston University. He is a co-author of the prize-winning social history *"Like a Family": the making of a southern cotton mill world* (UNC Press, 1987). He is the author of *Covering America: a narrative history of journalism*, which was published in the fall of 2011 by the University of Massachusetts Press.

Anthony Delano, PhD, MB (Comm), is a Visiting Professor at the London College of Communication and a former managing editor of the *Daily Mirror*.

Bridget Griffen-Foley is the Director of the Centre for Media History at Macquarie University in Sydney. Her most recent book is *Changing Stations: the story of Australian commercial radio* (UNSW Press, 2009), and she is now working on *A Companion to the Australian Media*.

Olga Guedes, PhD, is Senior Lecturer in Media Studies of the School of Arts and Humanities at Nottingham Trent University in the United Kingdom and a visiting professor of Media Studies at University of Fortaleza in Brazil. She is the author of *Understanding Alternative Media* (2008) and *Transnational Lives and Media: re-imagining diasporas* (2007).

Jairo Lugo-Ocando, PhD, is a Lecturer in Journalism Studies at the University of Sheffield in the United Kingdom. He is also a visiting lecturer at the Universidad de Malaga in Spain and a visiting Research Fellow at the Universidad Católica Andrés Bello in Venezuela. He has published *ICTs, Democracy and Development* (2009) and *The Media in Latin America* (2008).

Horst Pöttker is a Professor at the Institute of Journalism at the University of Dortmund. His teaching and research interests include journalism history, the language and style of journalistic genres, professional ethics, and research methods. He holds a PhD from the University of Basel and has taught at the Universities of Freiburg i.Br., Leipzig, and Siegen. During fall semester 2001–2 he was a visiting research scholar at the School of Journalism and Mass Communication, University of Iowa. In 2001 he initiated a debate on the National Socialist past of German communication science, which can be found at the home page of the Deutsche Gesellschaft für Publizistik- und Kommunikationswissenschaft (www.dgpuk.de). He is widely published on social, ethical and historical aspects of journalism including (with Hoyer) *Diffusion of the News Paradigm 1850–2000*.

Andie Tucher, an Associate Professor at the Columbia University Graduate School of Journalism, has been the director of the Communications PhD program there since its founding in 1998. Her book *Froth and Scum: truth, beauty, goodness, and the ax-murder in America's first mass medium* (UNC, 1994), a cultural and social history of the founding of the mass commercial newspaper press in the 1830s and 1840s, won the Society of American Historians' Allan Nevins Prize. Her current projects include essays on aspects of the evolution of the art of reporting in the late nineteenth century and a book about the intersections of history, memory, and storytelling in one family's 400-year-long American experience. Before coming to Columbia, Tucher spent 10 years in print and broadcast journalism. She earned her PhD in American Civilization from New York University.

Herman Wasserman is Professor and Deputy Head of the School of Journalism and Media Studies, Rhodes University, South Africa. He has published widely on media in post-apartheid South Africa, most recently the monograph *Tabloid Journalism in South Africa: true story!* (Indiana University Press, 2010) and the edited collection *Popular Media, Democracy and Development in Africa* (Routledge, 2011). He edits the journal *Ecquid Novi: African Journalism Studies*.

PREFACE

This special issue of *Journalism Practice* takes a carefully considered look at the various ways in which journalism uses history and historical sources, in order to better understand the relationships between journalists, historians and scholars of journalism. The idea for the project was developed by Martin Conboy, Professor of Journalism History at Sheffield University UK. I am very grateful to him for bringing together such a distinguished group of internationally respected scholars to produce this significant collection of original, research based essays which make a substantial contribution to our understanding of 'How Journalism Uses History'.

I would also like to offer thanks to Anthony Delano (London College of Communication) for his finely crafted and highly engaging Foreword and also to express my gratitude to John Nerone (University of Illinois, Urbana Champaign) and Debra Reddin van Tuyll (Augusta State University), for reading and offering helpful comments on all of the articles published here.

BOB FRANKLIN
Cardiff University, UK

FOREWORD

Anthony Delano

All journalists of a certain vintage remember newspaper libraries that could produce worn envelopes packed with cuttings on almost anyone and any event. They also remember news editors—and lawyers—reminding them that because something could be found in those clippings it was not necessarily right. Check, young reporters were told. And if there was time, check again. Such advice was never applied to the contents of the books many libraries would also come up with for "background". Hard covers signified authenticity.

That assumption was not always justified, particularly when an historian made tendentious use of similar clippings as a prime source or failed to evaluate them adequately. For the better part of a century the accusation that Spain had sunk the battleship *Maine* as one of the causes of the Spanish–American war of 1898 was accepted as an invention of the Yellow, i.e. popular, Press. Historians preferred the less sensational explanation of an accident on board, thus allowing several generations to be educated in the belief that the war had been popularised by a dodgy premise engendered by hysterical newspapers. Nearly a century later evidence emerged that the Yellows might actually have been right. *The Zimmerman Telegram*, a magisterial work by the queen of historians, Barbara Tuchman, is flawed by an account of Japanese incursions during World War One that depended on a fictitious account by a rogue journalist that, even at the time, was convincingly refuted.

Plenty of blame, then, to share between both occupations. In these and similar instances of inaccurate historiographic framing to which contributors to this issue draw attention it was historians who undertook the rectification. But instead of waiting for later scholars to question the accepted, journalists could just as easily have trawled through the same faded cuttings and seen a different image in the rear-view mirror. They did not do so because of an implicit demarcation: yesterday belongs to history. But, as the Hollywood re-makers like to say, what goes around comes around. Those stories and many more that were buckled into the protective armour of hard covers began as journalism. So, to twist Marx's overquoted aphorism into a new shape, journalism repeats itself first as history then as journalism again.

The distinction between practitioners was not always sharp. One of the earliest Journalism degree courses, at the University of Missouri in 1878, was taught in the History department, an arrangement followed in other places if only because academics were wary of letting a streetwise intruder run loose amid the ivy. Eventually, of course, American journalism teaching was all but subsumed in the great wave of academic enthusiasm for Mass Communication in which narrative was trumped by methodology, measurement and theory.

Journalism teachers who valued message more than media—scorned by media sociologists as Green Eyeshades—lost much of their independence. But a significant number of dissidents thought salvation could lie in a renewed alliance with History. Gene Roberts, a managing editor of the *New York Times* and a visiting professor at the University of Maryland, was arguing back in 1996 that history departments would make better partners in the study of journalism than "communications esoterica".

In the same decade, when the University of Michigan ended the autonomy of its Department of Journalism and absorbed it into Communication Studies, Jim Tobin, a *Detroit News* reporter with a PhD in history, explained why "the academy's attitude towards journalism usually ranged from vague distrust to outright contempt":

> it is partly motivated by a competition for cultural authority—a competition over who gets to speak the truth to the public. The academic who works on a single article for months believes not only that he simply knows more than a reporter writing for tomorrow's paper—which is usually true—but also that he holds to a higher standard of truth. His own motives are pure; the journalist's are commercial. Yet every day the academic realizes that he speaks the truth only to a small band of colleagues and mostly indifferent students, while the reporter speaks dreck to an audience of millions. So when it comes time to evaluate a journalism department, the academic says, "why should we teach students to do this shit?" (Carey, J. (Ed.) (1996) *Journalism Education, the First Amendment Imperative, and the Changing Media Marketplace*, Middle Tennessee University Press, p. 24)

Perhaps because Journalism wormed its way into British higher education rather later that in most countries, things worked out differently. The kind of academic misgivings Tobin described meant that some courses had to be labelled Journalism *Studies* but, if anything, Media Studies and Cultural Studies, or at least the parts of it that are not mere A-level material or just plain silly, are frequently incorporated into Journalism courses here, rather than the reverse. Without any ringing declaration being made, it seems accepted that journalism is *not* a communication medium but a process, a practice.

Another consideration in Britain is that History seems in danger of being downgraded, when not entirely abandoned, in secondary education and is losing ground at university level. Putting aside any consideration of how this might have come about, could it be time not merely to question the officers-and-men distinction between historian and journalist but for Journalism to come to the rescue of faltering History departments?

The ranks have never been entirely closed off. Distinguished academic figures like A. J. P. Taylor and Hugh Trevor-Roper, were happy to have the exposure—and the income—that came from servicing the popular prints, even when they were doing it to reinforce the prejudices of a proprietor-patron. Television studios seethe with ambitious history dons churning out programmes that are essentially journalism.

Meanwhile, as to the use Journalism should make of History (and historians), there no longer seems to be reason to accept that one begins only where the other ends. The contributors to this issue show what good stories there are to be found, even if they disturb audiences conditioned by historical myth-making. Today's research resources make it possible—even without Wikileaks—to mine raw sources, locate original material. Do what journalists are supposed to do: scrutinise, question, assess, report. Don't let them get away with anything.

HOW JOURNALISM USES HISTORY

Martin Conboy

The journal *Journalism Practice* has, since its launch in 2007, as one would expect from an interdisciplinary venture, adopted a laudably broad approach to exploring the complexities and variations in the practice of journalism. This has included the encouragement of a range of perspectives on the history of journalism. This themed issue of *Journalism Practice* aims to contribute to the scrutiny of journalism from both a professional and an academic perspective by exploring the ways that journalism deploys history and historical sources as part of its patterns of production.

History and Journalism: Setting the Context

As Journalism Studies continues to develop as a subject area throughout the world (Franklin, 2009; Tumber and Zelizer, 2009), journalism history is emerging as one of its most fertile sub-fields (Bingham and Conboy, forthcoming; Löffelholtz and Weaver, 2008; Zelizer, 2008). Burgeoning publications in the area, increased research students and curriculum enhancement have meant that there is a need for the subject to develop a stronger appropriation of its own historical base. If this historical work is to achieve its full potential, however, there needs to be a fuller and more consistent engagement with other academics studying the past: political, social and cultural historians in particular, but also scholars working in politics, sociology, literature and linguistics. There is, furthermore, an evident appetite in the humanities for such collaboration. In history there is an increasing preoccupation with language, discourse and identity; in literature departments, there is ongoing work on the journalistic output of prominent authors, and a growing interest in the ways in which categories of literary taste were shaped by public debate in periodicals; more and more politics scholars, meanwhile, are exploring the root causes of public apathy and disengagement in civic life as expressed in the output of news media, increasingly within a historical context. Diana Dixon, the compiler of an annual current bibliography on newspaper and periodical history since 1987, has noticed both the expansion in literature published in the area of journalism history as well as the wide range of disciplinary areas across which it is spread (Dixon 2003). The digitization of print and visual media archives has even since the publication of this survey, significantly extended the opportunities for such research.

Many of the core themes which inform history's engagement with journalism as a source were addressed at a one-day conference held at the University of Sheffield in September 2010 entitled "Journalism and History: Dialogues" as the inaugural conference of the Centre for the Study of Journalism and History jointly directed by the departments of Journalism Studies and History at the University of Sheffield.

Developing the Dialogue

However, while historians' increasing preoccupation with language, discourse and identity has encouraged them to draw increasingly upon journalism texts, there has been a relative neglect of the other direction of traffic in this dynamic; the ways in which journalism makes use of history. In some ways this is understandable given the apparent concentration of journalism on events in the contemporary world. Yet at a more considered level it can be observed how reliant journalism is on the markers of the rhythms of our experience of the everyday, in its routinization of anniversaries, obituaries, memorials and how certain of these experiences of the past are mediated by journalism as cornerstones in both editorial and national identities.

Studies of the processes and routines of journalism's engagement with historical sources can illuminate the sophistication of contemporary journalism as well as refreshing the rather clichéd "first draft of history" approach. In addition, it can provide further evidence for the claims made by Barnhurst and Nerone that: "history provides an indispensable tool for critiquing professional journalism by showing its contingency and entanglements" (2008, p. 17).

This special issue explores ways of conceptualizing the uses that journalism makes of history such as the commercial imperative of knowing about the past in planning for publication in the present; the uses of the *vox populi* as a historical resource and as a form of editorial credibility in establishing and maintaining a bond with the audience; the matching of particular journalism products within a particular historical frame as part of editorial identity; the past as a topic of conversation between editorial and audience in the form of readers' letters; the news media as recorders of a "common history". The contributors to this issue aim to set up more ambitious dialogues about using journalism both as a source for understanding the past, and for clarifying ideas about its role as constituent of the public sphere, through its discourse and traditions, in connecting contemporary audiences with history.

In the past, there was a tendency for other disciplinary areas to use journalism as a means to explore interests of their own without paying too much attention to the specifics of the medium they were exploiting (Tucher, 2007). This has begun to change with academics (and often journalists prominent among them) working within the field starting to develop historical accounts which foreground the nature and scope of journalism itself. In short, this special issue demonstrates a commitment to adding momentum to this trajectory from a professional as well as an intellectual perspective and add credence to something which is as much an intellectual sea change as a professional shift in the ways that journalists have come to appreciate the historical base of their own practice.

The contributions included here demonstrate a sample of the potential range of interest from a wide geographical and methodological perspective. They highlight academic assessments of the ways in which journalism uses history as a resource and, in addition, they draw upon the experience of former journalists who can reflect upon the processes at work within journalism's appropriation of historical sources as well as considering journalism's own past as a contribution to the evolution of journalism as a specific communicative genre. The special issue consists of six original and specially commissioned articles from distinguished journalism historians, many of whom have experience as journalists. These are complemented by an editorial essay and a foreword by a former journalist of some standing who remains highly active in debates around journalism education.

Horst Pöttker draws upon a rich, comparative framework of historical analysis to explore why contemporary German news media choose to focus increasingly on past events—here the National Socialist past. He argues that in the midst of the digital media upheaval, journalism must shift its emphasis from the rapid communication of mere news to other functions if it is to continue to make the world comprehensible to its public. Drawing upon history as a reservoir of potential knowledge enables journalism to provide a distinctive contribution to public debates and in doing so demarcates it from other more instantaneous information flows.

Andie Tucher provides a demonstration of how, at Columbia University, a journalism history elective enables students to consider the complexities and conundrums of their chosen profession; the achievements and also the mistakes of their predecessors; the contingency of conventions and the mutability of values, ideas concerning what journalism is for and how it should be judged. Drawing exclusively on journalism texts rather than secondary sources helps convince the students that the seminar will not directly contribute to getting them a job but it may encourage them to think more widely about what that job means.

Bridget Griffen-Foley explores some of the many ways history has been presented by Australian journalists and other media practitioners, focusing on the press and radio, since World War I. In doing so, she considers the role of journalism, and the media more generally, in the creation of a national narrative around Anzac Day; recognising indigenous dispossession; and facilitating the emergence of Australian public historians and intellectuals.

Christopher Daly provocatively sets two questions in dialogue to develop the debate about pedagogy and journalism's uses of history as this dynamic shifts over time. Are journalists always wrong? Are historians always right? Based on a successful university seminar at the University of Boston, this article sets out generic, professional and historiographical questions which centre on what happens when journalists "cover" an event or issue, then move on, leaving the field to later generations of historians who are left to enquire about what drives the process of historical revision.

Herman Wasserman evokes the presence of the past in contemporary debates within South African journalists' own self-perceptions. This article draws on semi-structured interviews with South African journalists to explore their attitudes towards the impact of South African journalism's history on current practices and professional ideologies. It aims to establish the ways in which the history of apartheid is used to make meaning in post-apartheid professional debates.

Jairo Lugo-Ocando, Olga Guedes and Andrés Cañizález combine to explore the extent to which journalists and news editors in Latin America from the late 1990s have been using history to frame the accounts and narratives in their news stories as a way of providing legitimacy to their political allies while undermining that of their foes.

Refreshing the National Narrative

So how does journalism engage with the past? The evidence of this special issue would incline us to conclude that it does so in a variety of ways, all of which clearly prioritize the need of news media to establish and maintain a bond with a specifically national audience. This might at first seem rather counter-intuitive as most definitions of journalism seem to suggest that it is in the privileging of the present and its concentration on novelty that journalism can be distinguished from other forms of communication. This concentration on the new is traditionally presented as its chief identifying feature over time. It purveys the latest information. Carey argues, however, that the symbolic function of journalism in establishing and maintaining communities has a more significant role than its informational component. Carey (1989) has argued that newspapers have always been more concerned with rituals of identity formation rather than any positivist contribution to knowledge about the world. He therefore sees news more as a cultural form, created by and for the bourgeoisie in the eighteenth century and one which set the template for developments to follow even as it broadened out its social and economic base, providing not raw information but drama; conflict between rival forces, not a world of fact impacting upon fact. He elaborates this "ritual" view over the "transmission" model of communication:

> The ritual view of communication, though a minor thread in our national thought, is by far the older of these views old enough in fact for dictionaries to list it under "archaic." In a ritual definition, communication is linked to terms such as "sharing", "participation," "association," "fellowship," and "the possession of a common faith," … a ritual view of communication is directed not toward the extension of messages in space but toward the maintenance of society in time; not the act of importing information but the representation of shared beliefs. (Carey, 1989, pp. 20–1)

Such a ritual view depends to a large extent on a reconstruction and reconfiguration of the past, drawing upon a wide repertoire of mnemonic devices to effect the continuity and coherence of that community through time. The symbolic construction of community highlighted by Carey implies that the representation of the past plays a significant part in establishing a community of the present, particularly when that past forms part of a continuity within a national narrative.

To probe the continued validity of Carey's break with the informational traditions of journalism, we might consider certain recent configurations of the past in the British press. Prominent among these are the anniversaries of the heroic acts of World War Two. These have become more pronounced over time with a stark contrast between the twentieth anniversary of the D-Day landings reported in June 1964 in the *Daily Mirror*, where the only mention of the significance of the day came on page seven in a short two paragraph piece complemented by thumbnail pictures of Juno Beach in 1944 under attack and two men playing boules in the present, with no celebrations or flag waving and without any of the massive coverage which has now become commonplace in that paper as elsewhere in the 1990s and early twenty-first century. The huge news media coverage of and contribution to the sixtieth anniversary of the D-Day landings (Conboy, 2008) are testimony to the increasing importance of the referent of World War Two as part of the discursive formation of Britain through a shared understanding of a version of its past. The D-Day commemoration enables the newspapers in Britain, in particular, to use the past to reinforce differing editorial and therefore market identities and yet these identities all share a common set of narratives and vocabularies around the meaning of the war for Britain. However, none of these anniversaries would make much sense if they were not more routinely embedded within historical frameworks and contexts. It is these contexts which allow cohesion within the imagined news media audience and which supplement the stylistic substance of the imagined community as it recreates its own position in the world as a reassurance that all is not being swept away in a tide of fragmented communication forms nor flattened into a globally homogenized cultural experience. Galtung and Ruge (1965) provide a long list of criteria against which news values were constructed and these include several which, in combination with each other, provide an irresistible preference for narratives of nation to become a favoured topic for news media coverage, especially so in a British context where the past is such an integral part of the national present. The categories of "meaningfulness", "consonance", "continuity", "reference to elite nations" and "reference to elite people" all contribute to the privileging of national representation.

Harcup and O'Neill (2001) have provided an update on these categories for the contemporary and take a more specifically British sample but they too demonstrate that even their more broadly defined news value categories of "relevance" and "follow-up" continue to contribute to how community, nation and patterns of familiarity are structured and how they depend on this sort of cultural congruence to retain the loyalties of a contemporary audience. This is something which cannot be taken for granted. It must be constantly reinforced within the news media which on account of their circulation in the discourses of the present, enable the past—albeit a highly selected version of the past in keeping with the editorial priorities of the present—to remain under the gaze of the contemporary audience. These building blocks of national narrative are already in circulation especially in an "old country" (Wright, 1985). England—and it is England that most "British" newspapers are centred on in their narratives of national identification—is old both in terms of its real geo-politics (Seton-Watson, 1977) and in its myths and metaphors (Smith, 1993, p. 15).

The past bleeds into the present as a routine part of the planning of the news when it comes to diary events, anniversaries, the advance writing of obituaries (the best example of the forward planning of the past!). These regular, cyclical events can be used for different purposes within the general context of the news as educational device; as cultural context, particularly to induct younger readers into communal memories; as an editorial identification of what is important to the paper's identity; as part of a broader identification of the national interest and national priorities regarding interpretations of the past. However, the selectivity and prioritizing of these national narratives mean that, as Renan (1990 [1882], p. 11) observed as long ago as the nineteenth century, forgetting is a crucial factor in the creation of a nation. Just what is remembered has as much to do with the frequent low-key allusions and appropriations of the myths and metaphors of the national past, the nation's "banal" history (Billig, 1995) as it has with the grand-scale reconstitutions of the great moments of history.

It is often correctly asserted that news consists of a perpetual present, a preoccupation with novelty. This used to be particularly accurate for news within the traditional newspaper as the privileged and sole purveyor of the latest information. However, as other news media forms became better communicators of the instantaneous, from radio to the Internet, newspapers have been steadily recuperating the past as an important part of their communicative armoury. This comes in addition to an increased propensity to analysis and opinion articles. There is currently more attention paid to events from the past and to examining the patterns of such events as a guide to the present than ever before. Sometimes this comes within the popular resonances of recent history and at other times as a demonstration that the didactic function of journalism is returning to a modern variant of its early Victorian "educational ideal" (Hampton, 2004) as readers are taught how they relate to their own national pasts and as newspapers continue to emphasize their role as "social educators" (Hall, 1975, p. 21).

The past is becoming more important for the news media in general as it provides an increasing opportunity to differentiate themselves from mere information providers. Historical context provides much of the added value of journalism as it competes with other communication genres. We might hazard a neologism and suggest, against the grain of another cliché, that context, rather than content, is really the king within the contemporary news media. New technologies heighten the ability of online news to direct us to historical contexts via hyperlinks and digitally stored archives. At the same time, print and television news provide a more prosaic engagement with historical contexts—from "viewspapers", incorporating more historical context to "contextualized journalism" (Pavlik, 2001, p. xi)—as vital adjuncts to the still important provision of information; information-plus, we might say. The past has never been more present in the news than in our current instantaneously mediated environment.

This article will look at some examples of how newspapers, in particular, frame history to maintain aspects of their editorial identity and rapport with audiences in the present. Framing theory, so potentially important to the selection and shaping of agendas of historical representation have, by the admission of the doyen of framing studies, Robert Entmann suffered from the tendency to ignore the variable of time (Entmann, 2010, p. 401; Entmann et al., 2009). He stresses the need for a reconsideration of the diachronic aspect of framing. This is of great relevance to the themes of this article and the following brief examples are designed to open discussions on how journalism uses a particular set of frames to represent a specific account of history both on special occasions and on an everyday basis, and how this combination of the extraordinary and the quotidian are combined over time to produce the patterns of newspapers' accounts of a national history. To support the arguments of this paper, an event was selected which was particularly resonant for the United Kingdom: the anniversary of the Dunkirk landings in May 2010. A small selection of newspapers were examined ranging from popular tabloids, the *Sun* and the *Daily Mirror*, to the middle-market tabloids *Daily Mail* and the *Daily Express*, through to the elite compact *Guardian*. There was not a huge amount of material but this is to a large extent because of the heavy concentration of commemorative content on what has become the biggest event of national memory, the D-Day landings (Hammond and Hoey, 2004). Nevertheless, there is still a familiarity in the representations which acts as a useful bridge to the more trivial echoes of World War Two a couple of weeks later as England once again expected a successful outcome to its football team's efforts in the World Cup. This thematic focus was held for a couple of weeks so as to see the ways in which the specifics of the memory or historical construction of war is used not only as an extraordinary celebration of a specific event but as a more routine trope of audience-identification. The importance of Dunkirk, within the wider discourses of the historical evocation of World War Two, in the mythical memory of Britain is hard to overestimate as it has given rise to so many stereotypes and idealizations of the British themselves as resistant to foreign invasion and maintaining an indomitable spirit in the face of adversity. Dunkirk also flatters a certain self-perception of the British that they are at their most valiant in defeat. Neither of these explorations is intended or designed to be exhaustive, merely indicative of wider patterns of representations of history in the press and particularly the national British press.

Dunkirk in the British Press: Popularizing the Past

The popular tabloid newspaper, the *Sun* covers the anniversary, albeit on pages 26–7:

> 70 YEARS LATER . . . THE FORGOTTEN VOICES OF DUNKIRK
> (*Sun*, 27 May 2010)

The article supplies a brief context to the events of 1940 and then a range of individual voices. This is a variation of the commonly used *vox pop*, here most definitely speaking as representatives not just of the "people" but as a wider embodiment of the nation itself. These act as a contrast to the memory of the actual voice of Churchill referred to here and the official history cited in the paper's coverage extracted from a recently published book entitled *Forgotten Voices of Dunkirk*. The article is complemented by four large pictures of troops being evacuated, sourced from the archives of the Imperial War Museum. Picture libraries are first and most commonly easy sources of corroborating information and illustration for historical pieces in the news but they can be so much more than that. As here, they act as authentification of the account being presented by the newspaper and act as a link to the real lives of the survivors of the war at the same time as they are amplifying the educational role of the national press.

The *Daily Mirror* rose to prominence as a modern tabloid newspaper during the war. Indeed, it has been described as acting during the war as "the Bible of the Services' rank and file" (Cudlipp, 1953, p. 136). It has Dunkirk on its front page on 27 May but only as an insert advertising a free-pullout souvenir of the *Daily Mirror* from 1940. It is relegated to the inner pages by the news of Cheryl and Ashley Cole's divorce details. Inside is a selection of front pages from the week of Dunkirk in 1940 including the reporting of Churchill's famous "We shall never surrender" speech. There is also a story which focuses on one veteran who had been on the *Lancastria* when it was sunk by German aircraft on 17 June. His parents thought he was dead until they saw his picture, face turned towards the camera in the *Daily Mirror* some weeks later as he climbed about a French trawler. The paper parades its own role in alerting the soldier's family to his survival: "My mum and dad thought I was dead . . . then they saw me in the Mirror" and features interviews with the soldier, Reg Brown, and other survivors as well as reproducing the photograph.

On the following day, the *Daily Mail* provides a story told through the eyes of veterans Walter Hart, 91, and Lionel Tucker, 93, and is to a large extent an exercise in contemporary, popular historical narrative:

> 70 years on, a tear for the heroes of Dunkirk
> The evacuation came after the speed of the German advance through Holland, Belgium, Luxembourg and France left hundreds of thousands of British and French troops trapped.
>
> The ships, many of them private fishing and pleasure boats, were drafted in to support Operation Dynamo, led by the Royal Navy. Between May 27 and June 4, 1940, 338,000 troops were rescued. (*Daily Mail*, 28 May 2010)

The importance of these witnesses to history is that their personal memories become entwined with historical memory on a national scale and this is orchestrated editorially on behalf of these "little men" of history. In their experience of such an iconic moment of the nation's history, they have become the subjects of Deep England.

To be a subject of Deep England is above all to have *been there*—one must have had the essential experience, and one must have had it in the past to the extent that the meaningful ceremonies of Deep England are above all ceremonies of remembrance and celebration (Wright, 1985, p. 85).

The use of veterans as proxy narrators of these heroic national tales is made more poignant as this generation of men and women become mere memories themselves. This is perhaps one explanation why the newspapers feel it is more important to establish their place in the national narrative with increasing coverage so that it is robust enough to be transmitted as myth when the lived experience and live recollection of that experience are no longer available.

In direct contrast, and on the same page in this newspaper, that same past can also be used as an acerbic commentary on the contemporary when the "fallen" of World War Two are deployed as an ideological counterpoint to the political priorities of a local council. In this way, the heroes of the war are used pointing both ways—to the past and to the present. This juxtaposition relates a story from Liverpool about the Council's decision to refuse funding for the Liverpool Military Show which included a memorial service to the "fallen" of the war. It is reported that the event failed to score highly on a "diversity scale" and events which were funded by the Council are listed as including: Gay Pride and International Day against Homophobia.

The *Daily Mirror* on 28 May provides a double-page spread (pp. 12–13) punning in popular tabloid fashion on the name of the French port:

Been there, Dun that
CHEERS AND TEARS AS THE 'LITTLE SHIPS' RETURN TO DUNKIRK 70 YEARS ON
(*Daily Mirror*, 28 May 2010)

Of course, the "little ships", an accurate description of the civilian craft which ferried the troops between the beaches and the larger naval vessels awaiting the troops in deeper waters off the French coast, add to the gallantry of the challenge and fit with the self-perception of the British as valiant against greater numbers.

To prove that this subject matter is predominantly but not exclusively the preserve of the popular tabloids, the elite newspaper, the *Guardian*, also provides an account, very much through the eyes of the veterans at the commemorative event, laced with explanations of the reasons why these numbers had been backed up against the channel by the advancing German army. Contemporary archive photos include an image of troops waiting to be evacuated on the beach in 1940 standing in seemingly endless lines.

Dunkirk veterans revisit scene of their salvation
(*Guardian*, 28 May 2010, p. 12)

The *Sun* provides a descriptive piece on the commemorative event, with photos of the veterans and the modern fleet as well as a thumbnail picture of the ships in 1940. The *Sun* fits the story's headline within the familiar contemporary tabloid idiom using the term "BRIT" as both signifier of national solidarity in the familiarity of its abbreviation, its space-saving properties in a bold headline and as a cross-reference to countless stories told as part of its nationalist editorial agenda (Conboy, 2006, pp. 49–50):

The bravest fleet
50 BRIT SHIPS SAIL TO DUNKIRK 70 YEARS AFTER SAVING 338,000
(*Sun*, 28 May 2010, p. 29)

The *Sunday Express* headlines its account of the celebrations:

The heroes return to Dunkirk beaches

Here, the "miracle of deliverance" is used as a direct quotation from British history's own man, Winston Churchill. Yet the story is still told from the eyes of veterans once again and in particular the account of the last surviving "skipper" of one of the "little ships", Alan Song. There is an accompanying full-colour picture of the veterans at the commemorative event of the beach at Dunkirk. This is complemented by an editorial which combines past and present on page 24, starting off with an imperative, an exhortation to its readers to bear witness to the myth in the present:

Recall the Dunkirk spirit

LET'S salute the men who 70 years ago sailed their "little ships" over to Dunkirk and rescued the British Army. Their extraordinary courage under fire turned defeat into victory and their bravery inspired the nation.

No wonder Winston Churchill said at the time: "We will fight in the fields and in the streets, we shall fight in the hills. We shall never surrender."

The Dunkirk spirit saw us through to victory and at times like this we could do with some more of it. (*Sunday Express*, 30 May 2010)

Once more we see the past used to reinforce the present as the spirit of the nation in adversity is more generally, even obscurely used to reinforce the necessity for this attitude to be drawn from the national reservoir in the contemporary world. Yet in stark editorial contrast, in the Comment section Peter Hitchens writes provocatively, as if taking the myth-making by the horns:

Dunkirk: Are we finally ready to face the truth?

I think enough time has passed since Dunkirk for us to admit the truth about it. It was not a triumph but a terrible national defeat—surpassed in the 20th Century only by the other Churchillian catastrophe of Singapore in 1942.

Having entered a war for which we were wholly unready, for a cause which was already lost, at a time we did not choose and with allies on whom we could not rely, we were flung off the continent of Europe in weeks. Only thanks to a double devil's pact did we survive as a nation.

We sold our economy and our empire to Franklin Roosevelt's USA, and we handed half of Europe to Joseph Stalin's homicidal tyranny. They won the war in the end, though we had to contribute many lives to their victory. Then we looked on as they rearranged the world.

Sooner or later, the fuzzy, cosy myth of World War Two and our "Finest Hour" will fade. We once needed to pretend Dunkirk was a triumph. If we are to carve our way in a hostile world, we now need to understand—as those who were actually on the beaches well knew—that it wasn't any such thing. (*Sunday Express*, 30 May, p. 33)

The irony is that despite this explicit reappraisal, the whole fabric of national newspaper coverage makes such an outcome all but impossible as it is as much at odds with both the myth-building of national narration as it is with the editorial strategies of the newspapers who are dependent on the maintenance of nation in order to preserve national readerships and therefore nationally based profits. As long as newspapers play their part in re-asserting the cycle of resonances for the contemporary world which commemorations of World War Two provide, there will be nothing like this reassessment. Seventy years on, if anything, the role of history in reinforcing a coherent story of national heroism and its relevance as an exemplar for the present is amplified more than ever even as the last survivors disappear. This is elaborated in a piece from the *Daily Mail* which perfectly captures the use of a particular set of historical narratives to support the contemporary editorial and political priorities of a newspaper; the past as a lesson for the present:

> **Bel Mooney**
> **Rekindling the Dunkirk spirit, 70 years on**
> I'M THINKING of Operation Dynamo, especially today, when 275 weary cyclists are riding into Dunkirk, wearing the distinctive dark blue, red and sky colours of Help for Heroes. On Monday they set out on the Big Battlefield Bike Ride 2010 to raise money for what has to be the coolest charity going.
>
> Operation Dynamo was the military codename for the evacuation of Dunkirk, which took place between May 27 and June 4 in 1940, after British troops were cut off by the German Army. Now, 70 years later, 275 human dynamos will be joining the townspeople of Dunkirk in a great celebration of the historic event which gave the English language that phrase which sums up courage and solidarity, "the Dunkirk spirit"...
>
> War is always with us, as the people who bowed their heads in Wootton Bassett earlier this week know well. So do those hardy souls who have raised sponsorship to ride 350 gruelling miles in five days through the battlefields of northern France, remembering the fallen—as well as men and women serving today... (*Daily Mail*, 29 May 2010, p. 51)

As the fervour of the commemorative events wanes, the launch of a set of stamps is a signal for one popular tabloid to provide a humorous context declaring:

> *We will never be licked..*
> *TRIBUTE IN STAMPS*
> **SEVENTY years on, these four stamps commemorate the bravery and spirit of the Dunkirk evacuation**...
> Royal Mail's Philip Parker said: "Few events in British history sum up the nation's resilience more than the miracle of Dunkirk". (*Daily Mirror*, 31 May 2010, p. 30)

History as Contemporary Context

For all the heroic resonances of the commemorative coverage, as noted above, national narratives and myths can only be sustained if they are put to daily use (Anderson, 1986). Only a few weeks after the sober and literal accounts of heroism at the Dunkirk evacuation, we can see references to World War Two used as complements to stories of much more contemporary appeal as we move from the tragic to the trivial. This is most marked, as one might expect, in the popular tabloids. There are martial allusions and specific historical references aligned to England's latest bid to win or at least progress in the football World Cup. On the front page of the *Sun* on 18 June 2010:

> On the 70th anniversary of Winston Churchill's historic speech, England's footballers must tonight give the nation...
> THEIR FINEST HOUR (and a half)

This has a context box on same front page explaining the relevance of the quotation to readers unaware of its significance: "just like Winston Churchill did with our forces on the eve of the Battle of Britain".

On page 3 of this edition of the paper we see the traditional Page 3 Girl deployed in the updated ironic commentary on the news, "NEWS IN BRIEFS", which trivializes both the half-naked women it presents as well as the editorially constructed commentary which she is claimed to be responsible for. Of particular note for our purposes is the reference to war-time heroism in terms of contemporary football with the addition of mock-classical allusions:

> Amy says England fans are right to turn to the words of war-time PM Winston Churchill to help inspire the team. She said: "Who could fail to be motivated by powerful Churchillian rhetoric, which has its roots in the oratory of ancient Greek philosopher Cicero?" [sic]

On page 4 in the same edition, the metaphorical is turned into the literal as 11 bulldogs are pictured in England kit under the command:

> Show us bulldog spirit, England

The connections between the mythologized heroism of the past and the expectations of the constructed national audience of the newspaper in the present is made explicit in its leading article which quotes from Admiral Nelson's famous signal at the Battle of Trafalgar:

> **Sun Says**
> England expects
> …The Sun's message to England echoes the call to arms 70 years ago today of that greatest of all leaders, Winston Churchill.
> **Let this be your finest hour—and a half!**

The *Daily Mirror* on the same day also feels the need to combine myth and contemporary national identification around football and uses "England expects" as an editorial headline but without any explicit historical references. Yet equally interesting is that deep, deep in the paper on page 31 is a piece on archival research from Cambridge University on the revisions Churchill made to the text of his most famous speech made on this day in 1940 complete with typed and hand-corrected reproductions of the archive material:

> FINEST TUNING
> **How Churchill agonized over inspirational speech**
> IT is one of history's most famous speeches—but newly released documents show how Winston Churchill agonized over his "Finest Hour" address to Parliament.

By the time of England's group game in the World Cup, the country was still reeling from the news of the new government's budget and the ultimate Churchillian rhetorical phrase was deployed to bring together a nation under threat on the front page of the *Daily Mirror* on 23 June 2010:

> **England go for glory—budget horror story**
> **BLOOD, SWEAT & TEARS**

—with each of the three main headline words illustrated by the face of first, manager Fabio Capello, second, star player Wayne Rooney, third, Chancellor of the Exchequer George Osbourne.

Another example of the confluence of the past and the present comes some weeks after but within the same echoing of the current economic and political crisis framed in terms of a crisis from the past. In the context of the Liberal Democrats' Party Conference scheduled for the following week, the *Daily Mail* on 17 September 2010 slipped in this historical comparison showing how the past can be used to frame the present for a national audience:

> It is worth remembering that 71 autumns ago government officials were struggling to persuade the public just how serious the situation facing Britain was.
>
> Historians have described that period as the "phoney war". But then in October 1939, the Royal Navy battle ship Royal Oak was torpedoed in Scapa Flow in the Orkneys and more than 500 men were lost. The brutality of war became horribly apparent.
>
> The summer of 2010 has witnessed a political phoney war. It is due to end over the next three weeks when everyone is forced to accept that hard times are here. At such a time the country needs our politicians—including you, Vince Cable—to rise to the occasion.

Here we have, incidentally, an example of the newspaper getting its details of the past wrong. The "phoney war" was not a retrospective construction by historians, rather it was very much a live political issue in 1940 as the United States in particular queried the extent of hostilities on the Western front. This was reported in British newspapers from political speeches made to US representatives by British politicians at the time. Between January and March 1940 newspapers as varied as the *Daily Mirror* and the *Manchester Guardian* were carrying Anglo-American debates about the "phoney war" in their pages.

Conclusion

The nation is demonstrated across these few examples as being an extremely malleable construct, from a rhetorical device calling for collectivity in the present, deploying real memories, archival materials or using metaphorical allusions to the spirit of the nation in a variety of contemporary circumstances. In these newspapers the "nation" has slid in its specificity as it embraces memories of the troops at Dunkirk who are most clearly identified in their heroism as "British", while the "nation" exhorted to do well in the World Cup is explicitly England! Churchill's "nation" has shrunk; his historically specific "Blood, Sweat and Tears" speech has become a transferable cliché. To return to Renan once more, a nation can be described as a large-scale solidarity, constituted by the feeling of the sacrifices that one has made in the past and of those to be made in the future (1990 [1882], p. 19). It is remarkable that British newspapers are more profoundly involved in these practices of national myth-making even at the point where technologically they appear to be most under threat of extinction. We might well call this a triumph of the cultural imperative in the face of their decline as a commercial proposition and indicates that historical contexts appear to form part of their viability as a form of social communication even as their cruder informational value might be disappearing. It is also remarkable that the words of a nineteenth-century historian can also ring so true to the twenty-first century. These two facts in combination indicate something of the continuing relevance of the ways in which journalism deploys history to maintain the coherence of its practice in the present.

REFERENCES

ANDERSON, BENEDICT (1986) *Imagined Communities*, London: Verso.

BARNHURST, KEVIN G. and NERONE, JOHN (2008) "Journalism History", in: Karin Wahl-Jorgensen and Thomas Hanitzsh (Eds), *The Handbook of Journalism Studies*, Abingdon: Routledge, pp. 17–28.

BILLIG, MICHAEL (1995) *Banal Nationalism*, London: Sage.

BINGHAM, ADRIAN and CONBOY, MARTIN (Eds.) (forthcoming) Special Issue: "History and Journalism: Dialogues", *Media History* 18(3).

CAREY, JAMES W. (1989) *Communication as Culture: essays on media and society*, Boston: Hyman Publishers.

CONBOY, MARTIN (2006) *Tabloid Britain*, Abingdon: Routledge.

CONBOY, MARTIN (2008) "A Tale of Two Battles: history in the popular press", in: Sân Nicholas, Tom O'Malley and Kevin Williams (Eds), *Reconstructing the Past: history in the mass media 1890–2005*, Abingdon: Routledge, pp. 137–52.

CUDLIPP, HUGH (1953) *Published and Be Damned*, London: Andrew Dakers.

DIXON, DIANA (2003) "Navigating the Maze: sources for press historians", *Media History* 9(1), pp. 79–89.

ENTMANN, ROBERT M. (2010) "Media Framing Biases and Political Power: explaining slant in news of Campaign 2008", *Journalism: Theory, Criticism and Practice* 11(4), pp. 389–408.

ENTMANN, ROBERT M., MATTHES, J. and PELLICANO, L. (1999) "Framing Politics in the News: nature, sources and effects", in: Karin Wahl-Jorgensen and Thomas Hanitzsch (Eds), *Handbook of Journalism Studies*, Abingdon: Routledge.

FRANKLIN, BOB (Ed.) (2009) "Tenth anniversary edition", *Journalism Studies* 10(6).

GALTUNG, JOHAN and RUGE, MARI (1965) "The Structure of Foreign News: the presentation of the Congo, Cuba and Cyprus crises in four Norwegian newspapers", *Journal of International Peace Research* (1), pp. 64–91.

HALL, STUART (1975) "Introduction", in: Anthony Smith, *Paper Voices: the popular press and social change, 1935–1965*, London: Chatto and Windus, pp. 11–24.

HAMMOND, PHIL and HOEY, JOAN (2004) *History as News: an analysis of media reporting of the fiftieth anniversary of D-Day, 6 May–7 June 1994*, London: London International Research Exchange.

HAMPTON, MARK (2004) *Visions of the Press in Britain, 1850–1950*, Urbana and Chicago: University of Illinois Press.

HARCUP, TONY and O'NEILL, DEIRDRE (2001) "What Is News? Galtung and Ruge revisited", *Journalism Studies* 2(2), pp. 261–80.

LÖFFELHOLTZ, MARTIN and WEAVER, DAVID (Eds.) (2008) *Global Journalism Research: theories, methods, findings, future*, Oxford: Blackwell.

PAVLIK, JAN V. (2001) *Journalism and the New Media*, New York: Columbia University Press.

RENAN, ERNEST (1990 [1882]) "What Is a Nation?", Martin Thom (Trans.), in: Homi K. Bhabha (Ed.), *Nation and Narration*, London: Routledge, pp. 8–22.

SETON-WATSON, HUGH (1977) *Nations and States: an enquiry into the origins of nations and the politics of nationalism*, Boulder, CO: Westview.

SMITH, ANTHONY (1993) "The Nation: invented, imagined, reconstructed?", in: Marjorie Ringrose and Adam J. Lerner (Eds), *Reimagining the Nation*, Milton Keynes: Open University Press.

TUCHER, ANDIE (2007) "Hope for Journalism History", *Journal of Magazine and New Media Research* 9(2), pp. 1–6.

TUMBER, HOWARD and ZELIZER, BARBIE (2009) Tenth anniversary edition, *Journalism; Theory, Practice and Criticism* 10(3).

WAHL-JORGENSEN, KARIN and HANITZSCH, THOMAS (Eds.) (2009) *The Handbook of Journalism Studies*, Abingdon: Routledge.

WRIGHT, PATRICK (1985) *On Living in an Old Country*, London: Verso.

ZELIZER, BARBIE (2008) *Explorations in Communication and History*, Abingdon: Routledge.

A RESERVOIR OF UNDERSTANDING
Why journalism needs history as a thematic field

Horst Pöttker

The article demonstrates that history is not only a legitimate but a necessary field of reporting which is becoming more and more important for journalism if the profession is to survive the challenges to its continuance from changes caused by the digital upheaval. There are five steps in argumentation: the first reconstructs the present transformation of journalism from the news function to the orientation function and identifies history as a reservoir of potential knowledge which enables an orientation in the present. This can be done by observing the present as a contrast to the past (critical mode), by looking out for similarities between the present and the past (analogical mode) or by reconstructing the present as something which has developed from the past (genetic mode). The following paragraphs concentrate on each of these three possible modes in which journalists can connect historical material to the present and thus do justice to the rules of topicality. This is demonstrated by examples of how the National Socialist past is and can be treated. The fifth step asks if journalists should trust themselves to interpret historical events. Here, it should not be forgotten that the choice of facts already implies an interpretation.

Introduction

Journalism must be up to date. Yesterday's newspaper is older than anything else. When looking for a binary code to delimit the social system of journalism (Blöbaum, 1994) from its environment, some theorists go as far as to say that topicality is the characteristic which distinguishes journalistic information from information in general. Does this mean that journalists should not report the past? Are historical topics a journalistic taboo just because topicality is obviously one of the most important journalistic qualities (Pöttker, 2000)?

These questions are already answered when we consider what topicality really means. A well-known definition says: it is not what is happening today but what is relevant today, that is topical. Relevant for the public, we should add. And, of course, the past can be equally relevant for the present-day public especially when it is problematic. For example, the National Socialist (NS) past is still particularly problematic because of the nature and the extent of the crimes committed in it. The German historian Christian Meier has recently demonstrated that the continuing public commemoration of Auschwitz breaks with thousands of years of experience in mastering a bad past by forgetting, simply because the incredible gravity of this violation of civilisation does not permit us to suppress or forget (Meier, 2010). If journalism, obedient to the rules of topicality, were to ignore the NS-past, its terrible consequences as well as its genesis, it would shirk the responsibility of remembering what, in this case, cannot be dismissed.

In a more general way, if it is the special duty of the journalistic profession to cater for publicness in modern, functionally differentiated societies, that is, to assure the optimal transparency of important occurrences and unsolved problems so that social self-regulation can function, then history is part of its legitimate thematic field because such occurrences and problems as require publicness result from the past.

I have already explored these arguments in a previous publication (Pöttker, 1997, p. 339). In this article I should like to go further and demonstrate that history is not only a legitimate but a very necessary field of reporting which is becoming more and more important especially for present-day journalism. I should like to show that journalism needs history as a subject context if it is to survive the threatening challenges to the continuance of the profession from the changes caused by the digital media.

This may sound surprising at first, for are not mobile telephones, satellite TV and Internet precisely those requisites which cast the spell of the here and now upon us all, members of the media public upon whose attention successful journalism, after all, depends and thus makes us oblivious of the past? This can hardly be denied and can tempt journalists or media managers to focus even more than previously on the troubled surface of present events.

However, the media are still full of historical subject matter and topics. Our everyday impression even indicates that the area of historical subject matter is expanding in the press, radio and professional Internet publications; this does not contradict the findings that show a decrease—at least in Germany, since the opening of radio to private and commercial suppliers in the 1980s—in the historical depth of daily current reports (Schatz et al., 1989). When I attempt, in the following section, to derive journalism's need for historical topics from trends emerging from the changes caused by digital media, we may well be in a better position to appreciate why the public expects journalists to take up historical subject matter more frequently.

Journalism in the Digital Media World: From the News Function to an Orientation Function

Among specialists, there is hardly any doubt that the journalistic function of transmitting news to the public is on the decline in the digital media world because quickly absorbed messages about the most recent events ("news") are no longer supplied by the mass news media but force themselves on the recipients from all sides. In order to find out how the German national football team played this evening in the world championship in South Africa, even in a distant holiday resort, I do not have to wait for the sports pages of tomorrow's newspaper. I encounter the results of the match automatically when I sit down at the hotel computer to send a last good-night message; the source of this information is not necessarily a journalistic one, probably, it is from FIFA itself. Or, on a train journey, I gather from the mobile phone conversation of a fellow passenger—my eavesdropping is unintentional but, due to the volume, unavoidable—with someone outside who is following a live report on TV that a lot of people have just been crushed because the crowds at the Duisburg Love-Parade panicked.

In the digital media world, a curious person need not buy a newspaper, switch on a news programme or be active in any way in order to obtain the desired news. Indeed, it is the other way round; someone lacking in curiosity who (just this once) wants to be left in peace and to ignore the world of events, catastrophes and other major occurrences must take action to protect himself from the (partially, at least) unrequested flood of information.[1]

It is obvious that, in this new media world, journalism, if it is to survive as a profession specialised in creating social transparency—a task which is in the interest of complex societies whose ability to regulate themselves depends on optimal publicness—will rely less and less and, eventually, not at all, upon its function as a transmitter of news, a function it has successfully been able to rely on for a century because it has had no competition in the world of traditional mass media.

The century in question began in the 1880s when the "inverted pyramid", a news form permitting and encouraging rapid reception and thus specially appropriate for conveying current events, together with the "headline" which also catered for the public's need for the combination of novelty and rapidity, became the accepted professional standard (Mindich, 1998; Pöttker, 2005a). The century of the news paradigm has come to a close (Høyer and Pöttker, 2005),[2] the ties between journalism and the news function have loosened since external non-journalistic communicators and communicator organisations have started to gain prominence and make use of the working techniques and presentational forms developed by news journalism, influencing public opinion according to their own political, economic, religious or scientific interests, and since everybody has, thanks to the digital media technologies, been able to tune into social communication without proportionally increasing their investment costs.

Obviously, in this situation, journalism must be on the lookout for new functions which, in their turn, are made more necessary by the task of maintaining publicness in the sense of social transparency. The little word "new" is, however, in this context, not precise and perhaps a misleading term. The other functions which should be considered and which journalism must rely on in the future are communicative achievements[3] which the information media have already placed at the disposal of the public but which, during the century of the news paradigm, did not in the main inspire the public to pick up the newspaper or turn on the radio.

One of these long secondary functions, the, up to now, second most important journalistic achievement after the news function, is to help the public to better understand its increasingly complex life conditions. Specialists call this the journalistic orientation function (Bonfadelli et al., 2005, p. 308), and although it has its pitfalls, which I shall discuss in a moment, I will follow the terminological convention for lack of a more appropriate expression.

Whereas the news function demands occurrences and the reduction of the interval between reporting and reported happening and requires brief presentation forms like "inverted pyramid" or "headline" which order things according to priority, the orientation function also permits subject matter which can be assigned to categories such as process, position, situation or relationship; the interval between what is to be reported and the report which will, eventually, require a closer investigation, can be longer; and in this case the longer forms of presentation are more suitable. These forms, which demand a thorough and, eventually, time-consuming reception, rely on communicative principles such as authenticity (report, feature), argumentation (commentary, analysis, discussion), suspense (story), human interest (portrait), and dialogistic (interview) (Bespalova et al., 2010).

The attentive observer of media development will notice that this journalistic future has already begun. As opposed to the general trend of the continual decline in the circulation of daily newspapers, it is—at least in Germany—weekly newspapers such as *Die Zeit* and the *Frankfurter Allgemeine Sonntagszeitung* with their sophisticated reflection, thorough investigation and literary quality which enjoy considerable increases in circulation.[4]

At this stage we must, however, say something about the pitfalls of the enticing expression "orientation". If journalism is, in the future, to rely less on the news function, this does not mean that it must revert to seeing itself as an "educator of the public" ("Schriftleiter und Verleger", 1934) as during the NS-regime or as "not only a collective propagandist and collective agitator but also a collective organizer" (Lenin, 1976 [1901], p. 11) as in the German Democratic Republic or the Soviet Union. Journalists are not educationalists. In certain respects their profession could even be considered the opposite of education because they must respect the maturity of their public in order to fulfil the task of publicness. The function of making the world understandable to the public is the journalist's particular fulfilment; a fulfilment gained not by explaining the world with a schoolmaster's pointing finger but by making complex conditions transparent and so helping the recipients towards their own understanding of this world.

An understanding of the world—what does that mean? Let us begin with the expression "world". This is what we call the vast all-embracing environment in which we humans live, out of which we fashion our lives and which we must cope with throughout our lives. The epistemological position of critical rationalism as developed by Karl Popper (1934, 1945, 1957) is based on the not provable assumption that there is a world beyond and outside human perception which human knowledge can never fully grasp because of the subjective limits of our sensory organs and our limited thinking and communicative abilities. This is referred to as the principal impossibility of objective knowledge but human knowledge can approach this world when communicating communities maintain an intersubjective process of research, and this process is determined by certain rules of factual and linguistic logic and directed towards the truth. I accept this assumption although it cannot be proved, and this has something to do with the pragmatic conviction of a teacher of journalists that his work would be in vain if professional journalism, which successfully masters the task of publicness, could not help the members of modern societies to cope better with the unwieldiness of their existing world, a world beyond subjective constructions.

To understand the expression "understanding", we must first get an idea of what the world is like. An obvious way of doing this is to make the conceptual distinction between what kind of environment human beings find without their own contribution and what emerges as the result of their own actions. As human beings come into the world as helpless, deficient creatures, they are obliged to fashion their environment themselves so that it basically provides protection for their young and enables their socialisation. The first, existing, part of the world, we call "nature", the second, anthropogenic part, we call "culture", to which not only material things such as tools, buildings or clothing belong but also the immaterial products of human activity such as values, norms or language.

As culture consists, not least, of a natural world shaped by human beings, this distinction can only be a conceptual one. Worldly things can often not be clearly placed on one side or the other. A garden is culture and nature at the same time and languages too are produced by human communities, as their global variety, their essential connection with socialisation, their mastery and their change throughout the ages show. But nature, too, plays its part and provides all human beings with a brain and speaking organs as biological equipment.

But let us keep to the conceptual distinction in order to understand what an understanding of the world means, an understanding to which journalism can contribute. As far as the understanding of the existing "natural" part of the increasingly complex world is concerned, it seems to be helpful if we know the set patterns which nature follows. Because such laws of nature exist and can be mathematically formalised, the course of natural events can be predicted, techniques for controlling nature can be developed and, not least, dangers like the threat of climate change or the global overexploitation of fossil energy resources can be recognised and reduced or even completely resolved. Good scientific journalism which helps the public to understand the world better, attempts to impart knowledge of the elementary laws of nature in a vivid way, to make the connection with environmental dynamics or bodily function clear, as well as to point out appropriate individual preventative health measures.

The "cultural" part of the environment which is the main concern of most journalistic departments—politics, features, local news and, to a lesser degree perhaps, finance and sports—is a rather different affair. Cultural events and phenomena cannot, being man-made, be expressed in set patterns and therefore can hardly be predicted; they are extremely variable, that is, they are not only divided among themselves, between societies and locations, but also subject to permanent and, compared with the development of the natural world, unequally rapid change.

The latter aspect should now be concentrated on. Cultural phenomena have come into being, they have a distinctive past, in other words, they have a history. To understand nature we must know the laws which make courses of natural events predictable. To understand cultural phenomena and events, which are barely predictable and in need of interpretation, we must understand their coming into being, their past. History as a subject has, for this reason, a constitutive significance for the arts and humanities, which Jürgen Habermas, in his opening lecture in Frankfurt, aptly named the "historical-hermeneutical" disciplines (Habermas, 1968 [1965]), as mathematics has for the natural sciences.

History is a reservoir of potential knowledge which allows the independent understanding of complex conditions as long as these conditions have been created by humans themselves. Or, put more briefly: cultural phenomena cannot be understood if we do not know how they came into being.

As journalism is developing from the news function to an orientation function it has the opportunity, by picking out and clarifying past events, of assisting the public to a better understanding of the cultural present, in which each recipient must fashion his or her life as an individual as well as in society. On the one hand, historical journalism can, by reconstructing historical changes, make the public aware of the contingency of contemporary cultural and political circumstances. In performing this function, it can strengthen the consciousness of freedom and also highlight the responsibility of the public. On the other hand, making history public with its presentation of the repeated pattern of cultural processes can also show the limits which the *conditio humana* sets for individual and socio-political structuring and thus point out to society the pitfalls and dangers of present options.

The latter is especially valid when conveying information about contemporary history such as about the NS-regime in Germany or Stalin's dictatorship in the Soviet Union. The US history theorist, Ernst Breisach, defends the work of historians since the postmodernists' loss of Utopia: "Still, even postmodernists shaped their visions of postmodernity according to one 'master lesson', the one that related which aspect of the past must be avoided from now on" (Breisach, 2003, p. 199). What Breisach says about academic preoccupation with the past also hints at the possibilities that historical reporting entails for the kind of journalism that sees itself less as a transmitter of news than as an informative supporter of orientation. This can be achieved by journalistic means such as visualisation if they are not used superficially or superfluously (Zelizer, 1998, 2001). What makes this attractive for a public, disorientated in the context of postmodernist complexity, is that knowledge and the impression of the past gives the public the chance to make sense of the present.

Because historical journalism—as opposed to the study of history—must be topical, its own logic of quality spurs it on not to deal with the past as a subject in its own right, as a certain positivist branch of historical studies would like, but to connect the past with the present.

The reference to the present is what Friedrich Nietzsche, in his time, saw as the value and practical use of history which, without this reference, would only be a heavy burden of knowledge (Nietzsche, 1874). The German historian Jörn Rüsen, whose thinking closely follows Johann Gustav Droysen's *Historik*, also written in the second half of the nineteenth century (Droysen, 1977), developed a similar idea with regard to the aim of historical studies in his theory of historical narration (Rüsen, 1990, pp. 153–230). Already, in the nineteenth century, Friedrich Nietzsche had asserted a distinction between various kinds of historical narration (Nietzsche, 1874). Both Rüsen and Nietzsche distinguished structural ways in which the past can be connected within the process of public communication. With the exception of Rüsen's "traditional" mode—the mode of deliberate creation of myths, which is inappropriate for history and modern historical journalism[5]—three similar modes are presented.

Where the present and the past are contrasted, both Nietzsche and Rüsen speak of the "critical" variant where the present is understood as an issue of the past, Nietzsche speaks of the "antiquarian" and Rüsen of the "genetic" manner of observing historical phenomena in a practical way. What Nietzsche calls "monumental" history is for Rüsen *cum grano salis*[6] the "exemplary" manner of historical narration. We could also refer to this as an "analogical" type of reference to the present.

All three types are appropriate not only for an academic presentation of historical findings that wants to offer socio-cultural benefits, but even more appropriate for the journalist eager to achieve orientation and for whom the topicality of his products, in this case, the reference of historical information to the present, represents a constitutive quality. We shall begin with the variant which both Nietzsche and Rüsen call "critical".

Critical Historical Journalism: Aims, Subjects and Problems

The critical mode of narration which journalists can choose when they treat historical subject matter helps us to understand the present by giving the reader or listener the opportunity to consider their own still unfashioned world as the opposite of the reported past. The contrast usually occurs when the description of past conditions confronts the public with questions of ethical interpretation (e.g. in the case of a fictional report about the burning of a witch at the beginning of the modern era). Critical historical journalism according to Nietzsche's or Rüsen's typology also means "putting your hand into history"[7] which, for example, permits the public to see in rapid economic or technological progress the sense of the present (e.g. by means of a statistically supported report about mass poverty and infant mortality in the nineteenth century); "critical", in this case, does not necessarily mean that it represents criticism of present-day society.

However, the critical narration type is not a mere negation of the past on the vaguely suggested background of the present but also the reverse process of confronting the public, through an affirmative presentation of the past, with the negative profile of the present (e.g. in a historical feature about the peak of cinema culture in the 1950s). Finally, we can imagine a balanced form of critical historical narration in journalism where the contrast is effective in both directions and loss *and* gain for the present with regard to the narrated past are made apparent. This was what, for example, Christian Graf von Krockow attempted in commentaries on the loss of the east German home country; he compared modern institutions which insure us against earthly risks such as fire, accidents or unemployment with the natural piety in East Pomerania before the Second World War which protected the inhabitants from the fear of death:

> We may well equip ourselves with nursing care insurance and many other such devices but they do not help us in our final hour. In Pomerania, however, they were prepared. The congregation sang . . . on the way to the cemetery, by the grave. And no one needed the hymn book because everyone long knew by heart the way he was being led. (Krockow, 2002, p. 70)

Such a weighing up of the ambivalence of progress in historical narration, which Krockow praised as the better alternative to glorification or condemnation (Krockow, 2002, pp. 304–7), could be seen as the climax of critical historical journalism because it follows the journalistic principle of impartiality and detachment. In practice, however, it does not often occur as, with regard to the critical variant of reference to the present, suitable subjects include those in which the violation of human rights and the commitment to their validity play a significant part. Human rights, formulated in 1948 by the United Nations, after the bitter experiences with the European terror regimes which provoked the Second World War, guaranteed by the written or unwritten constitutions of the western democracies and, subsequently, of most of the countries of the world, can be seen as a generally valid, super-national but also super-historical standard which enables us to compare past and present social conditions and to place them in an—eventually strongly contrasting—relationship to each other. As human rights provide, not only interculturally but also throughout time, the foundation for a normative dimension of understanding, they are predestined to serve journalism as an impetus to and a background for critical historical studies.

In Germany, the need to give a sense to the present and one which will liberate its people from the burden of the guilty past, is particularly great. This has led to a situation where, in the course of time, the increasing public and journalistic debate about the NS-regime but also the more or less public memory of the German Democratic Republic have reconstructed the conditions in the two German dictatorships as complete opposites. As a total contrast to the conditions in the Federal Republic of Germany, these two pasts are either rejected—or better, repulsed—by the majority of publications or nostalgically transfigured in the sense of a negation of the present by the past. The latter is achieved by minority media which, nevertheless, seem to reach up to a third of the East German population (Meier, 2010, pp. 127–56). Krockow's model of weighing up the ambivalence is seldom seen in German journalism and, as regards the two German dictatorships, is hardly appropriate.

Determined attempts at rejection, even the repulsion and repression of a bad past are understandable. Could we ever discover anything positive about six million murdered Jews or the 50 million dead in the Second World War or perhaps about the hundreds of people shot near the Berlin Wall? According to the normative rule of human rights this is morally impossible. All the same, the critical narration of a bad past can become problematic when it gets the upper hand and achieves a cultural hegemony which excludes the other modes of helping the public to understand the present by historical reporting. A striking example of this was the unanimous, negative, even outraged reaction of the German media and German politics to the speech of the parliamentary president, Philipp Jenninger, held on 9 November 1988 in memory of the pogroms against the German Jews 50 years previously. Because he did not content himself with moral indignation but went on to try to explain why so many Germans voluntarily followed the rule of the Nazis and participated in their crimes or passively witnessed them, public opinion, with very few exceptions, demanded and soon achieved his resignation. This was justified by an assertion which, even with only a superficial knowledge of the text, was blatantly false; he was accused of not being sufficiently detached from the NS-regime and, furthermore, of identifying himself with it. The true reason will have been the unwillingness of politics, the majority of journalists and the public to face up to the troubling fact of the collaboration of many Germans, that is, of their own parents and grandparents (Pöttker, 1989). The foreign press apologised to Jenninger a few days later when they discovered their mistake (Laschet and Malangré, 1989, p. 146). This apology has, up to the present day, still not been made in Germany.

When the critical variant of meaning given by historical information, with its emphasis on contrast and its insistence on moral detachment from the past, influences public opinion too much (Pöttker, 2005b), there is a danger that the continuity which links the present with the past will be ignored and finally denied. This brings us to the second mode of historical narration which journalists can use to provide the public with information needed in the search for the meaning of the present.

Genetic Historical Journalism: Aims, Subjects and Problems

What Nietzsche calls antiquarian history and Rüsen calls the genetic mode of narration is based on the certain assumption that the present is born of the past and then goes on to look for the birthmarks of the present and enquire what has remained—usually in a variation of the past.

The original premise is valid even beyond such a clear caesura as the total capitulation of Germany on 8 May 1945 seems to mark. But the people who had survived the NS-regime and the war had not vanished. People could not replace themselves. This means that their usual ways of behaviour and the interwoven patterns of their relationships, their values and norms could only change gradually and, possibly, as they are passed on across generations from parents to children, they have not yet completely disappeared.

An unusual but not fully unrealistic theory sees the moment of cultural historical change as late as the early 1960s. Here are one or two examples pertaining to the journalistic culture: during the period of the licensed press between 1945 and 1949, the western occupying powers really made an effort to give Germany, as far as possible, free media independent of the state. For this reason the media could publicise problems for which politics is responsible. In spite of this media policy, Adenauer's government met with a certain level of approval when it planned a law to control the press and create a pro-government television service. The latter was stopped by the highest court of the German Federal Republic in 1962, when, in the "*Spiegel*" affair, prominent journalists who had written an investigative story about the deplorable state of affairs in the army, were to have disciplinary action taken against them by the Minister of Defence, Franz-Josef Strauß (Pürer and Raabe, 1996; Seifert, 1966). An example of even more persistent traditional patterns of thought and behaviour, which continue into the present and by no means first began with Nazi rule in 1933,[8] is the almost total lack of correction columns or ombudsmen in the German press. The fact that mistakes, which must be admitted and corrected for the sake of credibility, are really inevitable for professional journalists working permanently under pressure of time, goes without saying in Anglo-Saxon countries with their long tradition of striving for independence and freedom of the press. In contrast to this, the authoritarian principle that only the most foolish lambs admit their own mistakes because, if they do, they will be led to the slaughter, is still part of the basic convictions of Germany's political and journalistic culture. These could be the subjects which a historically conscious, self-critical journalism could take up thus enabling the public to bring present and past together in a genetic manner.

However, the remains of authoritarianism no longer seem to be significant in Germany; in the 65 years since the end of the war, the country has progressed into a democratic civil society, a process which has had a profound effect on socio-cultural conditions. To name only one visible example, there are few flags and uniforms to be seen compared to almost any other country. Nationalism and chauvinism seem to confine their actions to the football arena.

I quote the example of the process of German democratisation, of which I have a good view as it corresponds to my present lifespan, to show that the genetic art of narration becomes less and less suitable with the increasing distance between the narrated past and the present it refers to. For example, it would not be a very productive journalistic idea to describe the Olympic Games of the ancient world as the origin of modern Olympics, or the Crusades as the predecessors of the missionary work of modern Christian churches. For this purpose, we should take a more comparative look and search for both similarities and differences. In the next section we shall discuss this as the analogical type.

If the theory is true that genetic narration is not suitable for events from the distant past but is especially suitable for the subjects of contemporary history, it follows that this mode of journalistically reconstructing the NS-past is becoming more and more questionable from decade to decade. This is all the more regrettable as the understandable dominance of the critical mode, with its power of disposing of the burden of the past, has long prevented and continues to prevent us asking the central genetic question: What relates present-day protagonists to this dreadful scenario of human creation? Which way of behaving, which could, due to the *conditio humana*, well be our own, caused Auschwitz and Coventry but also Dresden and Hiroshima? The answers are important if we want to avoid a repetition in the future.

The fact that the genetic mode becomes less practicable the greater the distance from the reported happening is by no means due to the *conditio humana*, defined as the constant natural conditions which provide a constant framework for our positive and negative potential. The factors which make that type of historical journalism obsolete which regards the past as the origin of the present can be traced back precisely to the changeability of cultural worlds, the relative freedom of human behaviour which makes us, as subjects, responsible for the consequences of what we have done or not done. For this reason, the possible danger of the genetic mode of narration is the overestimation of individual or social structuring potential.

If the genetic presentation of the NS-past aims at providing a meaning which obliges us to overcome still evident ways of behaviour upon which the Hitler-regime could rely, the historical comparison alone cannot give us an insight into the extent to which these ways of behaviour can be changed. Only an intercultural comparison can get rid of this uncertainty. It is not just by chance that, when mentioning examples of authoritarian residue in Germany's journalistic culture, I looked towards the Anglo-Saxon countries in order to show that, in the case of this heritage, we are not talking about unchanging facts of the natural world. Mere genetic narration cannot really show what chances of success can be expected as regards a change of problematic traditions or, vice versa, a conservation and restoration of proven relics of the past. Nietzsche, who called the genetic form of narration "antiquarian", speaks, in this context, of "antiquities" and their careful maintenance (Nietzsche, 1874). When discussing unchangeable continuity, necessary repetitive similarities between past and present, the third, exemplary or analogical type of narration is, however, the most obvious one.

Exemplary or Analogical Historical Journalism: Aims, Subjects and Problems

Nietzsche calls the exemplary manner of giving the public an orientation by historical journalism "monumental" history. This expression is, however, only appropriate to half of the facts of the case, for, in the search for the exemplary in the past, of analogies, of similarities with the present, journalists and scientists, who keep to the truth, make use not only of battles won, great moments, climaxes, but also, even more so in the sense of Ernst Breisach's formulated learning from history, of catastrophes and troughs of failure.

As far as practical standards are concerned by which highs and lows can be measured, I should like to refer to reflections on critical historical journalism made above. These standards differ from nation to nation and can even be structured in nationalistic opposition. For example, in London, Waterloo Station commemorates Wellington's final victory over Napoleon whereas, in Paris, we take the southbound train at the Gare d'Austerlitz which is named after Napoleon's greatest triumph.[9]

The fact that historical lows can be productive as regards the understanding of the analogical present is shown by much current journalistic practice during the global economic and finance crisis existing since 2008, which looked back to the exemplary economic depression at the end of the 1920s ("Black Friday"). At the same time, this example shows that the analogical type of narration demands not only the common ground of past and present but also the (gradual) differences, in this case, for example, the difference made by John Maynard Keynes' reaction to the great depression with his idea of compensation potentials by means of state economic programmes. Analogical historical journalism does not mean equation but orientation by means of comparison on the temporal axis. However, this does not exclude comparisons over long periods of time which show similarities related to the *conditio humana*. Because of this, the dynamic component, which shows the potential of freedom and responsibility, is here less evident than in the case of genetic narration.

To remind us of the NS-past, the analogical mode is the least suitable of the three narrative modes as it can lead to a misunderstanding of the present. Even after 65 years of westernisation and democratisation, German society will certainly not take an example either from structures directed towards an autocratic "Führer" personality or from everyday life during this regime characterised both by uniformity and by social isolation—to say nothing of the extermination of whole groups of people and of unscrupulously tyrannising other nations. When certain groups in the student movement of 1968 spoke, in the analogical mode, the historical mode based on common ground, of the "fascistic" Federal Republic, it was because fascism seemed to them a necessary terminal stage of capitalism and the Federal Republic had been, beyond doubt, from the very beginning a capitalistic society. This accusation gave an obviously false meaning to the present at that time although it must be stressed that it was an interpretation that was shared by only a minority of the students in revolt. For "how should we … explain the fact, that the world economic crisis, which began in 1929, helped Hitler to power but that the Western democracies that were far longer and far more strongly tied to capitalism, withstood? How can we interpret the fact that they finally took up the fight against tyranny and then unwaveringly fought it out?" (Krockow, 2002, p. 207). This is the question of a political scientist who experienced, and, to a certain extent, participated in the 1968 movement.

The disapproval of the analogical reminiscence of National Socialism is so extreme in present-day Germany that politicians who unwittingly make comparisons with that era are put under such strong public pressure that they (must) resign.[10] Some people interpret this phenomenon as a defence mechanism by which today's Germans fulfil their understandable desire to have nothing to do with National Socialism. There may be something in this interpretation but it overlooks the fact that, in Germany, it is indeed possible to concern ourselves publicly with the NS-past in a critical—and, in the meantime, a genetic—manner and that it is only statements in the analogical mode which are taboo in the official political sphere.

Like in many other things, our German love of basic principles makes us exaggerate when we completely taboo NS-parallels in politics, an exaggeration which can hinder precise debates because, at first sight, there seem indeed to be similarities which, when carefully compared, are shown to be differences. An example of this is the strong personalisation of politics, then as now, which, admittedly, as deeper analyses show, follows completely different patterns: whereas journalists were strictly forbidden to report Hitler's private life (Pöttker, 2006), so that the "Führer" could function as a virtual father and protector for everyone in the "national community", in modern democracies, politicians very much like the media to illuminate their private lives so that they can gain favour with voters as "people like you and me"; the construction of a "politician you can touch" at that time (in spite of his notorious fear of assassination attempts the "Führer" let himself be pawed in public and had red roses presented to him by young girls) stands in opposition to today's "transparent politician" (Pöttker, 1998).

Although the renunciation of NS-analogies might make such precise contemporary comparison more difficult, it seems to me to make sense, particularly during election campaigns where we can hardly expect exact argumentation, because a partial equation between present and this terrible past violation of civilisation leads, *nolens volens*, to a moral overloading of debates which blocks precise arguments even more.

Anyway, outside political discourse, or as far as it is led by journalists or scholars, everything out of the past—including everything out of the NS-past—should be an object at the disposition of the exemplary narrative form, whose core is the unchangeable *conditio humana*. This can first be ascertained by comparative historical studies over a long period of time.

On balance, the result is that we must be extremely careful when using the exemplary narration mode because it is prone to easily manipulated equations. The evidence of similarities can cover up the differences between present and past, which can only be discovered by a sensitively made comparison on the lookout for both opposing and common ground.

This does not mean that the analogical type of narration should be completely excluded for a particular historical subject or era. It would be a dubious affair if historical journalism were to press topics into a narration scheme in such a way as to make them lose important aspects. Exclusively critiquing National Socialism in terms of the present holds the danger, through the detached negation of the past, of forgetting to ask what still relates us today to that age of genocide and other crimes against humanity. The answers are given, in the first place, by the genetic type of narration which looks at this heritage so that the public can find out what parts of it must still be mastered. Here, intercultural comparisons are helpful.

However, historical journalism intending to offer the public an orientation concerning the NS-past cannot quite manage without the analogical type of narration. For this type permits the recipient to recognise what slumbers in himself and other people and what must be tamed so that similar actions are not repeated. The exemplary aspect of reporting on Auschwitz is a radical message directed towards a potential future which can still be avoided. The message shows that something has happened and can therefore happen again.

Are Historical Journalists Allowed to Interpret Historic Processes?

In the last few paragraphs, the question will have crossed the reader's mind as to whether historical journalism, in order to contribute to the understanding of the present, should be allowed to develop its own interpretation of the pasts it portrays or if it should rather confine itself to conveying historical facts. The latter proposition fits in with journalism's understanding of itself as a profession insisting on objectivity, and it allows the recipient—following Kant's definition of enlightenment (Kant, 1965)—to use his/her own understanding. The question has, up to now, been left unanswered, so that the reader can develop his/her own position. Now the question is to be answered as best we can.

First, we must ascertain that respecting the maturity of the public is one of the essential characteristics of journalism, one of the necessary factors which enable the creation of publicness in the sense of an optimal transparency of social processes and conditions. On the one hand, this respect permits journalists to confront their public with the whole truth without having to protect this public from damaging or superfluous information. Publicness is an aim *sui generis* which cannot be tied up to other aims and cannot be brought into line with well-meant schoolmasterly intentions. On the other hand, this respect prevents journalistic professionals and also professional historical journalists from dictating too much. In modern journalism, the point is not, as we might deduct from Niklas Luhmann's social theory (Luhmann, 1984), to convey a picture of the world which reduces its complexity but to make transparent the variety of what really is or was, so that the reader, listener or spectator can form his/her own idea of it.

This is also valid for the modern form of journalism that is turning away from the news function towards an orientation function. To be precise, historical journalism has the opportunity of contributing to the understanding of the complex present by conveying historical information without forcing interpretations on the recipient which are perhaps not immediately clear to him/her. For the three variants of a practical, present-based method of dealing with history, which, not by chance, occur in slight variations in the theories of historical narration from Nietzsche to Rüsen, are archetypical forms of comprehending which recipients practise consciously or unconsciously if they have enough knowledge of historical facts at their disposition. All this shows us that historical journalists should restrain themselves as regards their own interpretation of historical material and, instead, concentrate on reporting the material in the most complete and understandable manner possible.

The limits indicated by "most ... possible" in the last sentence are, indeed, a counter-argument. Complete reporting, we know, is not possible because we cannot say anything about what is unknown and therefore cannot be communicated. We must therefore assume that each collection of historical facts by academics or journalists is a selection out of the totality of what can be recognised and communicated; the selection has been made according to subjective criteria and therefore has interpretive components even when these are not named as a hypothesis, not to speak of them being tied up in an explicit context or a challengeable theory (Pöttker, 1980, pp. 77–179).

In other words, interpretations are *unavoidable* in historical journalism, too, but the more scientists and journalists—usually in good faith—profess to keep to the facts without adding any subjective ingredients, the less such interpretations can be criticised and discussed. For many years, for example, because nothing else was investigated and known, absolutely correct facts about the honourable activities of the German Army in the Second World War were reported. Their selection was based on the exculpatory theory or this theory had to be inferred from the public, that most Germans did not participate in the crimes of the NS-regime or that they were hardly informed about them. For a difference was to be made between the Nazi-clique and the SS, on the one hand, and the actually unsuccessful but, in the main, "clean-handed" majority of the soldiers, on the other hand.

This defensive reaction was certainly necessary for a long time, so that Germany could be rebuilt and could go through the process of democratisation with sufficient self-confidence. It came to an end in the late 1990s when the Reemtsma-Foundation's exhibition about the crimes of the army (Hamburger Institut für Sozialforschung, 1996,

2002) began to circulate, that is to say, since *other*, equally correct facts have become known which indicate the other interpretation of the guilty participation of normal Germans in the crimes. I do not quote the example to question the German effort to remember the NS-past but to illustrate the epistemological conclusion that reporting facts without interpretation is basically impossible.

Would it not be better if historical journalists disclosed their interpretations, if these are unavoidable, to the public? This would have the advantage of enabling the audience to look for alternatives and thus of maintaining the process of completion of factual knowledge. There is a lot to be said for this conclusion, which of course implies that historical journalists have a clear idea of their interpretations and interpretation patterns, an idea which, admittedly, requires an investigation of ourselves which is, if possible, unbiased and capable of distance and self-criticism. This can perhaps be expected rather from journalists than from historians whose academic careers, due to hierarchical structures in universities, demand adaptability, whereas journalistic careers, at least up till now in the prevailing news paradigm, are encouraged by news, antitheses and provocation.

However this may be, disclosing interpretations is also a way of showing respect towards the public's maturity. All the same, such interpretations should not, as all too often is the case in academic studies, project the image of dominant doctrines or any pretence at objectivity but should present themselves as what they are: subjective interpretations of collections of facts, interpretations which—not even historical journalism can escape the hermeneutical circle—in their turn have already served as a basis for the collection of facts.

Can or should historical journalists trust themselves to make their own interpretations? The argument that journalism should not, through the aid of orientation, anticipate the public's own understanding of the complex present, is just as plausible as the argument that subjective interpretations, which are unavoidable and inherent in each choice of facts, should not be concealed from the public. Perhaps a third idea can be of use to help us further, an idea which ignores neither of the apparently contrary positions and attracts our attention to one of the practical problems of the historical journalist's work: that is, the question of how a journalist, who wants to give the public assistance towards an orientation through historical reporting, *finds* his subject.

At first, it seems obvious that the search for a subject should begin in the present, by looking out for the versions of the past which could be linked to it in order to fulfil the topicality rule ("What is important today?"). In the routine of their rather unreflective daily work, editors usually make things easier and allocate tasks and authors according to possible contributions to jubilees and commemoration days: on 27 January they report on Auschwitz, on 30 January about the seizure of power by the Nazis, on 8 May about the capitulation, on 20 July about von Stauffenberg's assassination attempt, on 9 November about "Reichskristallnacht" and reporting is particularly intensive when the number of elapsed years ends with a zero or a five.

This practice not only makes work easier but is also journalistically and economically effective because all the media do it and thus the attention of the public is automatically fixed on it. At the same time, the commemoration day agenda has something artificial about it which only contributes to an understanding of the present where the latter is evoked by the media. In such a media society, peppered with artefacts, journalism which is professionally more reserved, more respectful of the public, more concerned about the transparency of already-existing realities can mean giving up the attractive routine of choosing a subject according to the date or a round anniversary (Conboy, 2007).

Instead, the historical journalist's subject choice could begin with reflections on which present events or conditions, not created by the media, correspond to pasts imparting knowledge which can contribute to their understanding, and which of the three modes of historical narration, in the specific case, is most suitable for the correspondence. Then, the same ritual will not be followed from year to year, of lamenting the crimes of the NS-regime on 27 January or 9 November but for example in the year 2000 the audience would have been informed correctly and comprehensively about the NS extermination system when government and parliament decided about the level of remuneration for the few surviving victims of forced labour;[11] in this case, the genetic perspective, which sees the present as a consequence of the past and derives a responsibility from it, is an almost automatic choice.

In such a way, not only finding and treating topics but also making the reasons for topic choice a subject of reporting in themselves, would be, in my opinion, one of the most significant measures of personal interpretation which a historical journalist can and must be trusted to make.

ACKNOWLEDGEMENTS

I wish to thank Anne Bunjes for help with English translation. Also quotations from German references are translated by her.

NOTES

1. This does not mean that in many parts of the world, where few people have access to computers, satellite TV and, least of all, newspapers, there is not an even greater problem as regards the inadequate provision of information. For example, in the 1990s in the Russian "Oblast" Perm, more than three-quarters of the families had no contact at all to the information media (Gladkov, 2002, p. 9).

2. Others also see that the century has come to an end (Weischenberg, 2010). I differ from Weischenberg's hypothesis insofar as I see, not the end of journalism itself and its task of publicness, but only the end of its connection to traditional professional indicators such as the news function and also the self-portrait of the impartial observer or all the standards which enable indirect financing of journalistic products through advertising revenues (Pöttker, 2010).

3. For example, the symbolic creation of community by (public) communication, on which James Carey (2009 [1989]) and in Germany Jürgen Habermas (1981) have pointed.

4. According to IVW, the circulation of the *Die Zeit* increased between the second quarter of 2007 and the second quarter of 2009 by 2.2 per cent, and the *Frankfurter Allgemeine Sonntagszeitung* even by 9.3 per cent.

5. Above and beyond the differences in the quality of topicality, science and journalism have a common tie to truth in their statements, i.e. they must be correct, intersubjectively verifiable through experience and their process of completion must be maintained by disclosing the criteria of selection as regards the knowledge or communication subject.

6. Rüsen considers namely that not only historic peaks but also the troughs can provide parallels to the present.

7. "Griff in die Geschichte" was a permanent historical section in a regional German newspaper in the 1990s.

8. This was chiefly made possible by Hitler's and Goebbels' skill in taking up such traditions for their own purposes.

9. Marengo, Austerlitz, Jena, Bir Hakim—the Paris Metro is full of victories. There are no defeats.

10. A well-known case is the resignation of minister of justice Herta Däubler-Gmelin in 2002.

11. See http://www.stiftung-evz.de/.

REFERENCES

BESPALOVA, ALLA, KORNILOV, EVGENIJ and PÖTTKER, HORST (Eds) (2010) *Journalistische Genres in Deutschland und Russland. Handbuch*, Köln: Herbert von Halem.

BLÖBAUM, BERND (1994) *Journalismus als soziales System. Geschichte, Ausdifferenzierung und Verselbständigung*, Opladen: Westdeutscher Verlag.

BONFADELLI, HEINZ, JARREN, OTFRIED and SIEGERT, GABRIELE (Eds) (2005) *Einführung in die Publizistikwissenschaft*, Bern: Haupt.

BREISACH, ERNST (2003) *On the Future of History. The postmodernist challenge and its aftermath*, Chicago and London: University of Chicago Press.

CAREY, JAMES (2009 [1989]) *Communication as Culture. Essays on media and society*, revised edition, New York and Abingdon: Routledge.

CONBOY, MARTIN (2007) "A Tale of Two Battles: history in the popular press", *Media History* 13(2/3), pp. 257–72.

DROYSEN, JOHANN GUSTAV (1977) *Historik. Band 1: Rekonstruktion der ersten vollständigen Fassung der Vorlesungen (1857), Grundriß der Historik in der Ersten Handschriftlichen (1857/1858) und in der letzten gedruckten Fassung (1882). Historisch-kritische Ausgabe von Peter Leyh*, Stuttgart-Bad Cannstatt: Frommann-Holzboog.

GLADKOV, SABINE ALEXANDRA (2002) *Macht und Ohnmacht der "Vierten Gewalt". Die Rolle der Massenmedien im russischen Transitionsprozeß*, Hamburg: LIT.

HABERMAS, JÜRGEN (1968 [1965]) "Erkenntnis und Interesse", in: Jürgen Habermas, *Technik und Wissenschaft als "Ideologie"*, Frankfurt a. M.: Suhrkamp, pp. 146–68.

HABERMAS, JÜRGEN (1981) *Theorie des kommunikativen Handelns*, 2 Bde. Frankfurt a. M.: Suhrkamp.

HAMBURGER INSTITUT FÜR SOZIALFORSCHUNG (Ed.) (1996) *Verbrechen der Wehrmacht. Dimensionen des Vernichtungskrieges 1941–1944. Ausstellungskatalog. 1. Auflage*, Hamburg: Hamburger Institut für Sozialforschung.

HAMBURGER INSTITUT FÜR SOZIALFORSCHUNG (Ed.) (2002) *Verbrechen der Wehrmacht. Dimensionen des Vernichtungskrieges 1941–1944. Ausstellungskatalog. 2. stark veränderte Auflage*, Hamburg: Hamburger Institut für Sozialforschung.

HØYER, SVENNIK and PÖTTKER, HORST (Eds) (2005) *Diffusion of the News Paradigm 1850–2000*, Göteborg: Nordicom.

KANT, IMMANUEL (1965) "Beantwortung der Frage: Was ist Aufklärung?", in: Otto Heinrich v.d. Gablentz (Ed.), *Immanuel Kant. Politische Schriften*, Köln and Opladen: Westdeutscher Verlag, pp. 1–8.

KROCKOW, CHRISTIAN GRAF V. (2002) *Erinnerungen. Zu Gast in drei Welten*, München: dtv.

LASCHET, ARMIN and MALANGRÉ, HEINZ (1989) *Philipp Jenninger: Rede und Reaktion*, Aachen: Einhard; Koblenz: Rheinischer Merkur.

LENIN, W(LADIMIR) I(LJITSCH) (1976 [1901]) "Womit beginnen?", in: Lenin, *Werke. Bd. 5, Mai 1901– February 1902*, Berlin: Dietz.

LUHMANN, NIKLAS (1984) *Soziale Systeme. Grundriß einer allgemeinen Theorie*, Frankfurt a. M.: Suhrkamp.

MEIER, CHRISTIAN (2010) *Das Gebot zu vergessen und die Unabweisbarkeit des Erinnerns. Vom öffentlichen Umgang mit schlimmer Vergangenheit*, München: Siedler.

MINDICH, DAVID T.Z. (1998) *Just the Facts. How "Objectivity" Came to Define American Journalism*, New York: New York University Press.

NIETZSCHE, FRIEDRICH (1874) *Unzeitgemässe Betrachtungen. Zweites Stück: Vom Nutzen und Nachtheil der Historie für das Leben*, Leipzig: E. W. Fritzsch.

POPPER, KARL (1934) *Logik der Forschung*, Wien: Julius Springer.

POPPER, KARL (1945) *The Open Society and Its Enemies*, London: Routledge.

POPPER, KARL (1957) *The Poverty of Historicism*, Cambridge: Cambridge University Press.

PÖTTKER, HORST (1980) *Zum demokratischen Niveau des Inhalts überregionaler westdeutscher Tageszeitungen. Wissenschaftstheorie und Methodologie—Normative Demokratietheorie— Quantitative Inhaltsanalyse*, Hannover: SOAK.

PÖTTKER, HORST (1989) "Mut zur Nüchternheit. Was Philipp Jenninger am 10. November 1988 wirklich gesagt hat—und warum er gehen musste", *Medium* 19(3), pp. 27–32.

PÖTTKER, HORST (1997) "Aktualität und Vergangenheit. Zur Qualität von Geschichtsjournalismus", in: Günter Bentele and Michael Haller (Eds), *Aktuelle Entstehung von Öffentlichkeit. Akteure—Strukturen—Veränderungen*, Konstanz: UVK Medien, pp. 335–46.

PÖTTKER, HORST (1998) "Hitler zum Anfassen. Personalisierung von Politik am Beispiel des Rundfunkjournalismus im NS-Regime", in: Kurt Imhof and Peter Schulz (Eds), *Die Veröffentlichung des Privaten—Die Privatisierung des Öffentlichen*, Opladen and Wiesbaden: Westdeutscher Verlag, pp. 210–24.

PÖTTKER, HORST (2000) "Kompensation von Komplexität. Journalismustheorie als Begründung journalistischer Qualitätsmaßstäbe", in: Martin Löffelholz (Ed.), *Theorien des Journalismus. Ein diskursives Handbuch*, Wiesbaden: Westdeutscher Verlag, pp. 375–90.

PÖTTKER, HORST (2005a) "The News Pyramid and Its Origin from the American Journalism in the 19th Century", in: Svennik Høyer and Horst Pöttker (Eds), *Diffusion of the News Paradigm 1850–2000*, Göteborg: Nordicom, pp. 51–64.

PÖTTKER, HORST (2005b) "Öffentlichkeit/Öffentliche Meinung", in: Siegfried Weischenberg, Hans J. Kleinsteuber and Bernhard Pörksen (Eds), *Handbuch Journalismus und Medien*, Konstanz: UVK, pp. 329–33.

PÖTTKER, HORST (2006) "Journalismus als Politik. Eine explorative Analyse von NS-Presseanweisungen der Vorkriegszeit", *Publizistik* 51(2), pp. 168–82.

PÖTTKER, HORST (2010) "Der Beruf zur Öffentlichkeit. Über Aufgabe, Grundsätze und Perspektiven des Journalismus in der Mediengesellschaft aus der Sicht Praktischer Vernunft", *Publizistik* 55(2), pp. 107–28.

PÜRER, HEINZ and RAABE, JOHANNES (1996) *Medien in Deutschland. Bd. 1: Presse*, Konstanz: Ölschläger.

RÜSEN, JÖRN (1990) *Zeit und Sinn. Strategien historischen Denkens*, Frankfurt a. M.: Fischer-Taschenbuch.

SCHATZ, HERIBERT, IMMER, NIKOLAUS and MARCINKOWSKI, FRANK (1989) "Der Vielfalt eine Chance? Empirische Befunde zu einem zentralen Argument für die 'Dualisierung' des Rundfunks in der Bundesrepublik Deutschland", *Rundfunk und Fernsehen* 37(1), pp. 5–24.

"SCHRIFTLEITER UND VERLEGER" (1934) *Kölnische Zeitung mit Handelsblatt*, No. 204, Abendblatt, 23. 4.

SEIFERT, JÜRGEN (Ed.) (1966) *Die Spiegel-Affäre, Bd. I: Die Staatsmacht und ihre Kontrolle; Bd. II: Die Reaktion der Öffentlichkeit*, Olten and Freiburg i. Br.: Walter.

WEISCHENBERG, SIEGFRIED (2010) "Das Jahrhundert des Journalismus ist vorbei. Rekonstruktionen und Prognosen zur Formation gesellschaftlicher Selbstbeobachtung", in: *Krise der Printmedien: Eine Krise des Journalismus?*, Berlin and New York: De Gruyter Saur, pp. 32–61.

ZELIZER, BARBIE (1998) *Remembering to Forget: Holocaust memory through the camera's eye*, Chicago: University of Chicago Press.

ZELIZER, BARBIE (Ed.) (2001) *Visual Culture and the Holocaust*, Piscataway, NJ: Rutgers University Press.

ARE JOURNALISTS ALWAYS WRONG?
And are historians always right?

Christopher B. Daly

This piece focuses on a seminar which is currently taught at Boston University which draws on the insights of a conference held at the same university in autumn 2009. The conference brought together leading historians and journalists to explore the ground shared by the disciplines and, it is fair to say, sometimes divides them. The article argues that there is much need for an approach which draws on the strengths of both traditions while remaining aware of the shortcomings of each discipline. Drawing on debates within the historiography of both journalism history and mainstream history, it demonstrates the intellectual underpinning of the seminar which aims to point students to a wider array of the challenges, successes and reversals experienced by journalists and historians. It hopes to provide a method of investigating core questions about the journalism of the past in order to better inform the practice of journalism in the future. Furthermore, it extends this ambition to providing a collegial model for the exploration of other societies or periods of time which can be adapted at other universities.

Introduction: Are Journalists Always Wrong?

That is a question that I raise, only half in jest, in a new seminar being offered at Boston University. The seminar represents the fruits of a conference held on our campus in the fall of 2009 in which we brought together panels of accomplished journalists and historians to explore common ground. Much of the discussion focused on shared concerns involving research and writing, since both fields involve the creation of non-fiction texts for an audience of some size.

Part of our discussion extended to teaching. I pursued that discussion with my colleague Bruce Schulman, who is a historian, an Americanist, and chair of the Boston University History Department. The two of us—one a former journalist and current professor of journalism, the other a prominent historian—began to zero in on the question of what happens when journalists "cover" an event or issue, then move on, leaving the field to later waves or generations of historians. We wanted to know what drove the process of historical revision. (We also wanted to know whether any students shared our interests, and we were not sure through the many months of planning.) Eventually, we decided to examine about a dozen major events in US history. First, we looked at each one through the lens of the journalists of the period, those reporters who wrote what has been called "the first rough draft of history" (Shafer, 2010). Next, we looked at those same events through the lenses of the historians who followed and wrote the subsequent drafts. We decided that this might make for a lively course.

The Institutional Context

At Boston University, the president and provost have embarked on a campaign to encourage interdisciplinary efforts of all kinds. So, based on our joint interest in the issues and on our school's manifest support for inter-disciplinary work, we launched the course for the Fall semester of 2010. Hoping to encourage discussion, we organized it as a seminar, with a target enrollment of 20 students. We allocated 10 seats to the Journalism Department and 10 to the History Department, and we hoped to get a mix of graduate students and advanced undergraduates. In the end, we came very close to those targets.

In the readings we have used and in the discussions in class, we have found a familiar dynamic: journalists report some version of the facts, and then after a few years, historians take charge and set about working over the ground already covered by journalists. Often, after the passage of decades, the original version is hardly recognizable.

A Version of History in the Press

One case in point, among several, involved the war fought in 1898 between the United States and Spain. The first version of this historical episode, now largely discredited by scholars, was written by the newspapers themselves. The headliners in this tale were Joseph Pulitzer, publisher of the *New York World*, and William Randolph Hearst, his arch-rival and publisher of the *New York Journal*. Their newspapers were initially credited—and blamed—for fomenting the war. By the late 1890s, the two publishers were locked in a furious circulation war, throwing all their ingenuity and resources into devising more and more dramatic, shocking, and scandalous headlines, culminating in a set of practices known as "Yellow Journalism" (Campbell, 2001; Hamilton, 2009).

The publishers' eagerness for war is best illustrated in the year or two preceding the official declaration of war by the United States. Hearst and Pulitzer both sent correspondents to Cuba, literally looking for trouble, which they readily found (Lubow, 1992). Correspondents described the brutal treatment of Cubans by their colonial occupiers, including the use of "concentration camps" to round up and subdue Cubans.

In the summer of 1897, a story unfolded that met the publishers' needs exactly. A young woman named Evangelina Cisneros (invariably described as "raven-haired"), the daughter of a jailed Cuban rebel, was thrown into prison in Havana, on the grounds that she had dared to defend her honor against a rapacious Spanish colonel. Hearst's *Journal* editorially demanded her release—in headlines, news stories, line drawings, and editorials. Hearst personally led a campaign for her release, ordering his correspondents around the United States to call on prominent women to sign a petition to be sent to the Queen Regent of Spain.

From Hearst's point of view, the Cisneros story became more appealing when the Spanish refused to release the young woman. The editor dispatched a reporter named Karl Decker to Cuba, equipped with bribe money, and Decker managed to help the damsel escape to New York, where she could be feted and displayed. That allowed the *Journal* to crow, in decks of headlines arrayed as an inverted pyramid:

MISS EVANGELINA CISNEROS RESCUED BY THE JOURNAL.
An American Newspaper Accomplishes at a Single
Stroke What the Best Efforts of Diplomacy
Failed Utterly to Bring About in
Many Months.

Similarly, when a "visiting" US battleship, the USS *Maine*, blew up in Havana Harbor on February 15, 1898, both of the Yellow papers jumped to the conclusion that the deed was the fault of Spanish saboteurs. Even over the objections of the ship's captain, Pulitzer and Hearst presented the sinking of the *Maine* as a work of Spanish perfidy and called for the United States to retaliate. Just over two months later, the United States declared war on Spain.

According to the newspapers themselves, the cause of the war was their own coverage of Spanish abuses. In the first draft of this history, the Yellow papers rushed to take credit. A few days after the declaration of war, Hearst's paper even ran the following gloating headline:

HOW DO YOU LIKE THE JOURNAL'S WAR?
(*New York Journal*, May 1, 1989, p. 1)

For decades, that view prevailed. As late as 1947, it was at the heart of the analysis of the war presented by Stanford University historian Thomas A. Bailey in the chapter about 1898 in his book, *A Diplomatic History of the American People*, long a standard work. But by the 1960s, that interpretation was coming under attack. One milestone was the publication of the work of the Cornell University historian Walter LaFeber, who argued for an economic interpretation of the motives of US policy-makers in his 1963 study, *The New Empire: An Interpretation of American Expansion, 1860–1898*. Yet another approach emerged in the 1990s from the "culture studies" movement when Kristin L. Hoganson published her study of the war of 1898 titled *Fighting for American Manhood: how gender politics provoked the Spanish–American and Philippine–American wars*. She attributed the war mainly to the perception among that generation of American men of a need to assert their masculinity by going to war. In the later tellings, the activities of the Yellow Press fade or disappear altogether. In this episode, as in many others, the pattern is clear: journalists present one version of events, only to see that draft corrected, revised, or reinterpreted by historians.

Thus, the question persists: Are journalists always wrong?

Are Journalists Always Wrong?

In one, perhaps trivial, sense, the answer is obviously, No. Collectively, journalists gather, check, and disseminate vast amounts of information, ranging from the week's menu in the local school cafeteria, to the closing price of a share of stock, to the outcome of a football game, and on to topics that are more complicated and even interpretive. If one measure of the "rightness" of journalists is factual accuracy, then it must be acknowledged that most of the material in most news stories is right, at least in the sense that it is "not wrong." Most stories, after all, are never corrected because the factual material contained in them was accurate to begin with. They stand *un*-corrected.

Moreover, there is another sense in which journalists are "not wrong." That is, an old newspaper or news broadcast (like almost any text) can be used by a skillful historian as a source of *inadvertent* testimony about all sorts of things. Most journalists do not set out to provide a window into the workings of their society for the benefit of historians who will come along hundreds of years later. Yet, their work can serve that very purpose. For example, any historian who reads newspapers from the eighteenth or nineteenth century quickly realizes that even if the newspapers are inaccurate about this or that detail, they are unerring in their power to reflect the zeitgeist of their era.

Historians of the Press

As several leading historians have emphasized, newspapers reflect their societies even as they shape them. David Paul Nord (2001) has argued that early newspapers played a key role in building communities by giving readers common materials to reflect on. Michael Schudson has shown how newspapers embodied the competitive, commercial spirit of the nineteenth century, until a cultural shift sent many editors in search of a more professional mode in the twentieth century (Schudson, 1978). And James Carey, in defining the social role of newspapers in history, identified them as carriers of "consciousness *in* the past"—as opposed to contemporary historians, who one would expect to have a consciousness *of* the past (1974, emphasis added). "**When we study changes in journalism** over time, we are grasping a significant portion of the changes that have taken place in modern consciousness since the Enlightenment," Carey wrote in a landmark essay.

Indeed, in this sense, journalists *cannot be* wrong. Readers who skim just a few old stories can quickly see answers not only to the question of what happened on a given day but also to questions the journalist was *not* asking himself or herself:

- What does this society consider important enough to write about and pay for? In the early eighteenth-century newspapers, there is evidence that the topics people would pay to read about included piracy in the Atlantic trading world and legislative proclamations. A century later, news of the captures of runaway slaves swelled in frequency and in poignancy.
- How does the journalist conceive of the basic work product called a story? Early newspapers in America were often discursive, and even epistolary. Later, they became more partisan and eventually more dispassionate and "professional."
- What attitudes are prevalent about topics like race, class, gender? Some subjects, of course, remain so taboo that they never appear in the "public prints."
- What is the quality of the "public sphere" created by the uncoordinated actions of hundreds or thousands of journalists, each following his or her own lights?

These are subjects that every journalist "testifies" about through the work itself, even if the journalist never self-consciously tries to penetrate or analyze the surrounding society. This is one reason why many historians, especially social historians, are so intent on finding newspapers from the era they are studying and so happy when they find them. Wittingly or not, journalists always provide material that reflects *something* about their era.

More common, though, are those instances where journalists *are* wrong in a significant sense. One category of significant journalistic error involves information that has been suppressed. The history of the Cold War, for example, is rife with instances where one or more governments deliberately withheld information for years. The gradual release of

Soviet archives and the sporadic revelations of programs like the Venona Project (Haynes and Klehr, 2000) have given historians access to documents that while sometimes problematic, were not even available to journalists of the 1940s and 1950s. Journalists cannot be blamed for failing to report secrets, but their work in such an area is still incomplete and therefore misleading.

The Russian Revolution: Reassessment of Journalism's Role

Another category of journalistic error involves a more serious failure by journalists themselves—the sin of omission. A dramatic case that we examine in our course involves coverage of the Allied invasion of the new Soviet Union almost 100 years ago. In a little-known but far-reaching episode, US and British leaders decided to invade Russia—their recent ally in the Great War—in 1918 and stayed for almost two years (Knightley, 2004 [1975]). Few Americans ever heard of this mission, nor did they ever find much useful information about Russia in their newspapers during the war and for many years afterward. During the fateful convulsions of the Russian Revolution and its immediate aftermath, American journalists failed their readers—with few exceptions, miserably. Most simply failed to show up; most of the rest willfully misinterpreted the things they saw and heard.

Initially, czarist Russia had been a participant in the Great War, fighting against Germany from the start in 1914. As the war dragged on, however, Russian sentiment turned against the Czar, the entire Romanov family, and the war. In the spring of 1917, the Czar was overthrown, and that fall the Bolsheviks—led by Lenin and Trotsky—toppled the new government and began installing the Communist dictatorship. In the spring of 1918, the new Soviet government in Moscow negotiated a separate peace with Germany, based on the communist view that the war was a brawl among capitalist powers.

American publishers—successful capitalists themselves, for the most part—did not generally consider the Russian Revolution a big enough story to bother covering. As a result, their papers did little to inform Americans about the new society forming in the old Russia—neither the idealism of some of its followers nor the brutality of most of its leaders. The coverage only worsened in the following months. When the Soviets dropped out of the war on February 12, 1918, American newspapers denounced the move as a double-cross to the Allies (who would now have to bear the full brunt of the German military machine on the Western Front), and some went so far as to suspect that the Bolsheviki were really German agents. Aside from the young American John Reed, the correspondent for the socialist magazine *The Masses* and author of the classic book *Ten Days that Shook the World*, there were almost no American correspondents present in Russia to do any first-hand reporting (Reed, 1919). In their absence, American papers felt free to run stories predicting the Communists' imminent demise.

On the whole, the reporting in America about the Russian Revolution and the Allied expedition was so deplorable that it prompted a remarkable study by two young journalists the following year. They epitomized the drive to professionalize American journalism that was then gaining ground in the United States in the new university-level journalism programs at Missouri and Columbia, in the fledgling professional organizations like Sigma Delta Chi (which became the Society of Professional Journalists), and in the emerging trade press. The leaders of this movement, usually well-educated and ambitious young journalists, were dissatisfied with the field's raffish and blue-collar milieu; they wanted to set standards and measure performance. Among them were two of the most ambitious of the new professional journalists, both working at a remarkable young magazine of progressive outlook called *The New Republic*. One of the authors was Charles Merz, a Yale University graduate who later worked as a reporter at the *New York World*, then became the influential editor of the *New York Times* editorial page during World War II and the Cold War. The other author was Walter Lippmann, a Harvard University graduate who went on to become the most prominent and respected US journalist of the middle twentieth century, the country's unofficial foreign minister, a prolific author, and a syndicated whirlwind (Daly, forthcoming, chap 8). In August 1920, they teamed up on an impressive pioneering work of journalism criticism, which appeared as a supplement to *The New Republic* headlined "A Test of the News" (*The New Republic*, August 4, 1920).[1]

Lippmann and Merz conducted a comprehensive analysis of the coverage of Russia from the news pages of the *New York Times*, looking at more than 3000 news stories from March 1917 to March 1920. By design, they ignored the newspaper's editorials and focused exclusively on what should have been factual news accounts. They asked a very simple question: in light of the already known facts, how reliable had the reporting been just a few years earlier? From a reader's point of view, how factual and useful was it? In their judgment, the coverage was almost ludicrously bad.

To illustrate their point, the authors cited case after case where the *Times* correspondents were fanciful at best or deluded at worst. "News reports in 1917, 1918, 1919, and early 1920 that the Soviets are about to collapse, or have collapsed, or will collapse within a few weeks is false news," they pointed out, at a time when the regime was consolidating the power that would endure for most of the century. In the 24 months between November 1917 and November 1919, Lippmann and Merz documented 91 occasions when the *Times* news pages "stated that the Soviets were nearing their rope's end, or had actually reached it" (*The New Republic*, August 4, 1920, p. 10).

Four times Lenin and Trotzky were planning flight. Three times they had already fled. Five times the Soviets were "tottering." Three times their fall was "imminent." Once, desertions in the Red army had reached proportions alarming to the government. Twice Lenin planned retirement; once he had been killed; and three times he was thrown in prison (*The New Republic*, August 4, 1920, pp. 10–11).

Such coverage, which borders on farce, would have been hilariously bad but for one fact: the treatment of Russia by the Wilson administration during this period and the coverage of Russia by American newspapers affected relations between both peoples and their governments for the next 75 years or so. Again and again, the coverage in the *Times* featured wild speculation, blatant wishful thinking, and unsourced diplo-military mumbo-jumbo. In the end, Lippman and Merz concluded the typical US correspondent in Russia was about as useful as "an astrologer or an alchemist" (*The New Republic*, August 4, 1920, p. 42).

At root, Lippmann and Merz found that US reporters were too credulous, too tied to official sources, and too willing to write what they hoped rather than what they saw. "From the point of view of professional journalism the reporting of the Russian Revolution is nothing short of a disaster. On the essential questions, the net effect was almost always misleading," they wrote (*The New Republic*, August 4, 1920, p. 3). In the period in 1917 between the overthrow of the Czar in March and the success of the Bolsheviks in November, Lippmann and Merz found a cheerleading quality in the coverage: the new Russian government would stand firm with the Allies against Germany and never seek a separate peace. Even after Lenin and Trotsky came to power in the fall, the optimism kept up—not just in isolated mistakes but in dozens of front-page stories:

WE CAN DEPEND ON RUSSIA . . .
(*New York Times*, August 9, 1917, p. 1)

RUSSIA WILL FIGHT ON . . .
(*New York Times*, August 15, 1917, p. 1)

In the months following the Bolshevik victory, the collapse of the new regime was likewise predicted—regularly and confidently. Thus, it came as a substantial surprise to American readers when the Bolshevik regime survived and signed a peace treaty with Germany in February 1918.

Allied leaders suddenly sensed a new threat, and the coverage nimbly changed direction. Following the separate peace signed by the Bolshviks, the dominant theme in the US coverage turned to the German Peril. Germany no longer faced an army in the East, so the path was clear for German expansion as far as India or even Japan; besides, without having to fight the Russians any more in the East, Germany could now throw its full might against the British, French and US troops on the Western Front. Logic dictated that the Allies open an Eastern Front themselves, by invading Russia. They did so, in several places. Then came the armistice, and with it any further rationale for positioning foreign troops on Russian soil expired. Just at that moment, however, the coverage revealed a new menace: the Red Peril. Three days after the armistice, the *Times* offered these headlines:

BOLSHEVISM IS SPREADING IN EUROPE;
ALL NEUTRAL COUNTRIES NOW
FEEL THE INFECTION
(*New York Times*, November 14, 1919)

What had been described not much earlier as a bankrupt system on the verge of collapse was suddenly rampant. With the new threat came a new rationale for the Allied invasion. From three directions, British, American and other troops, linking up with leaders of various White Russian military units, attempted in 1919 and 1920 to march to Moscow and depose Lenin. In each case, the *Times* correspondents foresaw ultimate victory—right up until the moment of defeat.

Part of the reason that the *Times*' correspondents may have been able to sustain such high morale is due to the fact that they were not slogging through Siberia with the counter-revolutionary armies. Far from being "embedded" with the expeditionary forces, most of the correspondents were hundreds, or thousands of miles away. Judging by the datelines on their dispatches, they were quite toasty and safe in Moscow, Paris, and London. For example, Lippmann and Merz cite this story from the spring 1919 offensive, touting the progress of Admiral Aleksandr Kolchak (who, although a Navy man, was not leading the White forces in a land campaign):

KOLCHAK PURSUES BROKEN RED ARMY
London, March 26 (via Montreal)—The troops of the Kolchak government who pierced the Bolshevist front on a thirty-mile sector on March 11, continue their progress and the position of the Bolsheviki is precarious . . .

Within months, the admiral had fallen back a distance of some 2000 miles. (In fact, there was also a fourth invasion of the Soviet Union—heading south from Archangel—but

Lippmann and Merz simply threw up their hands on that one. The news blackout was so effective about the US Russian Expedition that there simply were not enough stories to analyze.)

Part of the problem, the authors wrote, involved the reporters' methods. Time and again, the sources of the dispatches from Russia were not only unidentified, they were so vague as to be barely worth mentioning: "allied diplomatic circles," "well-informed diplomats" or simply "It is understood . . ." or, perhaps the ultimate, "It is asserted . . ." How could anybody ever check these reports? How could these sources (if they even existed) or the reporters themselves ever be held accountable? Another shortcoming that Lippmann and Merz could have stressed more was the failure of those reporters to get out of the diplomatic swirl and go see things for themselves. A week or two of eye-witness reporting could have cured most of the worst stories. Ultimately, Lippmann and Merz concluded that "the professional standards of journalism are not high enough" and were not being enforced strictly enough.

If only the US correspondents had been as definite about a remedy as they were about the diagnosis. Among the results of such reporting were the chronic misleading of the American people. In the ensuing confusion, the government vacillated between a *laissez-faire* attitude toward Moscow and a secretive invasion. Another result was the poisoning of US–Soviet relations: the Soviet leaders could see for themselves that the capitalist powers had tried to overthrow them, and they could read for themselves that the capitalist newspapers had gone right along with the program.

From this episode it is clear to see that journalists can indeed be wrong at least some of the time. Moreover, when they are wrong in ways that are not trivial, those errors or omissions can in fact be quite consequential. Such errors can distort contemporary perceptions of politics and society in significant ways, and they can put the first few squads of historians on the wrong track. These are the cases that compel the process of revisionism.

On the other hand, it must be noted that there are cases where an original work of journalism resists revision for good reason. One example we consider in our class is that of John Hersey's classic work *Hiroshima* (1946). Is there anything "wrong" with it that must be corrected? Is it missing something important that has subsequently come to light? Has something else happened that makes us put Hiroshima (the event) in a different light? Is it no longer a singular episode of world-historical significance? The answer to all these questions appears to be no. Hersey appears to have been especially well prepared for the assignment. He had spent years working as a journalist for *Time* magazine and for the *New Yorker*, practicing the skills of interviewing and reporting. He was also an accomplished novelist, having won the Pulitzer Prize for fiction for his wartime novel, *A Bell for Adano*. In *Hiroshima*, he combined meticulous, first-hand reporting with the novelist's techniques of scene-setting and character development to create a masterpiece of non-fiction narrative. The book has been in print continuously for more than 60 years. In 1999, *Hiroshima* was judged the greatest single work of journalism in America in the twentieth century (Barringer, 1999).

Hersey did something quite innovative by the standards of American news-writing. He told the story of the Hiroshima survivors entirely from their point of view. As readers, we experience the day much as if we were standing right behind the survivors, passing through each scene in sequence. Almost never does Hersey break from that narrative perspective to pull back to the typical journalistic perspective of the distant, neutral observer. Instead, he presents a tight-focus, ultimately human answer to the question: what is it like to live through the worst violence the planet has ever known?

It was his use of such literary techniques that prompted some later critics to hail Hersey as the true inventor of the "New Journalism" that burst onto the American scene in the early 1960s (Weingarten, 2005). Hersey showed other journalists that it was possible to use literary techniques while sticking to matters of fact.

Historians have, of course, pursued the general topic of the atomic bombing at the end of World War II. Books have been written examining and debating the process that yielded the decision to drop the bombs and on many aspects of the world-changing event. But no significant effort has been put into revising Hersey's coverage of the question of what the experience of being bombed felt like and meant to those who survived it.

In a few cases, we have been forced to address a variation on this theme: are there times when historical revision is counterproductive? Sometimes the answer seems to be yes. There are instances when revision distorts the journalistic record or introduces error. Consider the curious case of America's third president.

A New Species of American Journalist: Callender

In the late 1790s, Thomas Jefferson was in the thick of the maneuvers that produced the "party system" of politics and governing in the United States. But at the beginning of the new nation, there were no political parties to speak of. Indeed, the founders, in writing the Constitution in 1787, had not even mentioned the word "party" in the document, reflecting the prevailing hope that permanent divisions—or "factions"—would not exist.

Into that vacuum stepped newspaper editors (Pasley, 2001). As Jeffrey Pasley has shown, editors played an indispensable role in building the parties, at a time when they had no legal existence, no rolls of registered voters, no slates of candidates, no nominating conventions, no money—none of the trappings of the full-grown political party. In the absence of the machinery of partisan electioneering, newspapers were the means for letting readers know which candidates held which views. By endorsing a candidate, or simply by informing readers whether a candidate was a Federalist or an Anti-Federalist, newspaper editors began to give voting an ideological coherence that it would otherwise lack. In turn, the nascent parties enlisted newspaper editors to help spread their views and tout their candidates. In the first few decades of the United States, partisan papers even printed ballots that voters could fill out and take with them to the polling places.

Like many of the other Founders, Jefferson was working hard to promote himself and his views, sometimes using a political ally as his agent and often enlisting a newspaper editor as his cat's paw. In one case, though, a cat's paw turned on Jefferson and mauled him. That was Jefferson's experience with one of the most vicious and dangerous of all the partisan writers and editors: the hard-drinking Scottish immigrant James Thomson Callender, perhaps the ultimate example of the partisan polemicist and scandal-monger, a mutant offshoot of the new species of American journalist then emerging at the dawn of the era of the Party Press.

Callender had a nose for trouble. Born in Scotland in 1758, he worked for a while as a clerk, got fired, and took up the cause of Scottish nationalism, quickly becoming a militant. In 1792, he was charged with sedition. Hunted by the Edinburgh deputy sheriff, Callender bade farewell to his wife and four children, and fled to America. He arrived in Philadelphia in May 1793—alone and nearly penniless. Within months, he was offered a job reporting on the debates in the Congress for the *Philadelphia Gazette*, which gave him a toe-hold. Soon, Callender's family had crossed the Atlantic and joined him. Struggling to make ends meet, he moved his family onto Philadelphia's docks and began drinking heavily.

Nevertheless, he managed to make himself useful to the Republican cause, writing pamphlets in support of Jefferson and his allies. In July 1797, Callender tackled one of the stars of the Federalist camp, Treasury Secretary Alexander Hamilton. In a lengthy pamphlet, Callender revealed that Hamilton had transferred money to a convicted swindler named James Reynolds, insinuating that Hamilton and Reynolds were scheming to speculate in Treasury certificates, which were under Hamilton's supervision. The charge forced Hamilton to defend himself, but his reputation was ruined and his career, effectively, capped.

In the aftermath of his victory in the election of 1800—which featured the first peaceful transfer of power between political parties—Jefferson faced the novel issue of how many positions in the national government should be taken away from their Federalist occupants and turned over to Republicans. One of those who came calling after the election was none other than Callender, who had his eye on the plum position of postmaster in Richmond, Virginia, but Jefferson sent him away empty-handed.

Callender set out to get even. He promptly switched parties, and, in February 1802, he became a partner with a Federalist editor in running the *Richmond Recorder* newspaper. Callender assigned himself the job of bringing down Jefferson. Acting on the basis of rumors that he had picked up from anonymous sources, Callender let fly in print with the accusation that Jefferson had engaged in sexual relations with one of his slaves, later identified as Sally Hemings.

> It is well known that the man, *whom it delighteth the people to honor*, keeps and for many years has kept, as his concubine, one of his slaves. Her name is SALLY. The name of her eldest son is TOM. His features are said to bear a striking though sable resemblance to those of the president himself . . .

The Federalist press had what it was looking for. The story was repeated in other newspapers, sometimes accompanied by lurid speculation about the "black Venus" at Monticello.

As for Callender, he was nearly finished. Having set the bar in the practice of scandal-mongering about the sex lives of the president, his own life quickly went downhill. In December, he was the victim of a public beating and again succumbed to his great thirst. The following summer, in July 1803, during another of his periods of heavy drinking, James Callender was found floating in Virginia's James River, dead at age 45.

Callendar was highly partisan and sloppy, yet he was almost certainly correct about Jefferson. In Callender's case, however, subsequent generations of historians revised his reporting into oblivion. He was denigrated as a scoundrel and relegated to the dustbin. It may be worth noting that he was not actually *refuted* (in what journalists would call a "knock-down") so much as he was denounced, pooh-poohed, or ignored. Captivated by their own admiration for the Founders, the eminent American historians—white men all—built Jefferson into a paragon, tailored for each subsequent period (Malone, 1948). Eventually and very gradually, the process of revisionism began to take hold. In 1974, historian Fawn Brodie published a best-selling "psycho-biography" of Jefferson that was the first book to take the Jefferson–Hemings liaison seriously (Brodie, 1974). Brodie, the first female scholar to tackle the controversy, made a much bigger impact on the public than she did on the historical profession. Most scholars continued to defend their conception of Jefferson's honor by minimizing or rejecting the Hemings tale (Ellis, 1997).

In 1997, the scholar Annette Gordon-Reed took up the case. She brought a unique set of credentials: she was not only a historian but also a lawyer; she was not only female but also African-American. In her *Thomas Jefferson and Sally Hemings* (1999 [1997]), she presents an argument, almost like a pleading in a lawsuit, asking readers to treat the evidence in the matter more fairly than most historians had done to that point. Gordon-Reed argued, *inter alia*, that historians should stop granting all white witnesses more credibility than all black witnesses. Looking at all the evidence in this new light, she made a persuasive case.

Still, skeptics wanted convincing evidence. That came in the following year, when white descendants of Jefferson and black descendants of Hemings underwent DNA testing that indicated an overwhelming likelihood that Jefferson had been the father of at least two of the Hemings descendants. The new, scientific finding not only vindicated Brodie, it also vindicated Callender—the drunken, "irresponsible," partisan journalist of nearly 200 years earlier. In the end, it turned out that the initial reporting was on the right track and that racial and ideological assumptions sent historians off on a lengthy detour. The truth was there all along, but historians willfully did not see it.

Are Historians Always Right?

The Jefferson–Hemings case prompted us to turn the debate around and ask another question: Are historians always right? In one sense, of course, the answer is obviously not. Some historians make errors some of the time. There is another sense in which historians are not always right. That is evident from the fact that some historians revise others. Indeed, in this sense, one might conclude that historians are *never* right.

Both fields have some common properties: they have a methodology for approximating truth. In journalism, the methods for approaching the truth are manifold: they begin with the process of editing and the discipline of competition with other news sources. They involve devices to insure independence and to avoid conflicts of interest. They include transparency (ideally) about methods and sources. They ultimately involve legal and even criminal sanctions. If a journalist makes a factual assertion that is both false and damaging to an individual's reputation (and causes some measurable harm), then the journalist can be sued in civil court for libel. In rare cases, if a journalist divulges certain kinds of military or state secrets, the journalist can be tried in US criminal courts for espionage or perhaps even treason.

In the historical profession, the mechanisms for approaching the truth are somewhat different. They typically begin with a lengthy, formal apprenticeship that culminates in a doctorate degree. They extend to academic tenure, a system that is intended to guarantee the scholar's independence. At the heart of the discipline's practices are those associated with publication: peer review, inclusion of scholarly devices such as endnotes, and the system of reviewing new books. In the United States, historians appear in court so rarely (as defendants) that it is not really relevant to consider legal sanctions. In both cases, though, it may be that both journalists and historians face the same ultimate bench of justice: the evolving judgment about their work as expressed by their readers. In the end, readers far outnumber editors, and due to their collective wisdom, it is difficult (though not impossible) to mislead them for very long.

Common Ground or Friction?

Yet, for all that historians and journalists have in common, there is also a fair amount of skepticism and even mistrust between the two fields. Historians, in my experience, read a lot of journalism in the natural course of things. They also rejoice when they can find any kind of periodical in the era they are studying. Yet, historians often look down on journalists as a grubby, ignorant lot—hustlers who exaggerate, prevaricate, or simply scavenge randomly from what Thoreau called each day's "froth and scum" (Thoreau, 1991 [April 24, 1852]).

Journalists, for their part, commonly read a lot of history—sometimes as recreation, sometimes as "background" for their work. Yet, many journalists feel a sense of unease about history, especially about the variety of history now practiced in universities. They feel disappointed by many academic historians, blaming them for taking perfectly good "material" and robbing it of its inherent color, drama, and energy in order to advance ceaseless argument or "discourse."

Part of the friction between journalists and historians arises from the fact that the two kinds of non-fiction inquiries are asking different questions. Almost always, the foremost question on the journalist's mind is: what happened? At the moment when that question is first asked, no one knows the answer, so any answer—even one that is fragmentary, tendentious, or clichéd—can be quite compelling. Immediately after that question has been answered, however, the answer begins to lose salience. The characteristic response of the professional journalist is to move on to the next event or surprise, leaving others to mull over matters of interpretation and analysis.

Most of the time, historians are not particularly interested in the question of what happened, because it is pretty well settled by the time they begin their work. They are more interested in asking how or why something happened, or what it means for later generations. Questions of interpretation and causation are paramount. Regrettably, these concerns are often emphasized over the story-telling skills of scene-setting, character development, and textual pleasure.

Conclusion

Thus, we might hazard a reply to the question, Are journalists always wrong? That answer seems to be: yes, no, and it depends. At the same time, we might venture to ask, Are historians always right? In that case, the answer also seems to be yes, no, and it depends.

In our course at Boston University, we believe we have begun to explore these questions in a way that can be easily adopted to fit other universities and to study other societies or time periods. In our experience to date, the effort to examine journalism and history at the same time is both fruitful and suggestive. By putting both fields into a critical tension with each other, we can point our students toward a wider array of challenges, successes, and reversals experienced by journalists and historians. We have tried to put these two fields—each proud of itself and wary of the other—into a more productive relationship. Such a cross-disciplinary approach holds out the promise of illuminating something essential about both journalism and history.

NOTE

1.   At this vantage point, of course, it seems a fair question to ask: how well were Russian readers served during the same period by their own news media? Such a study remains to be done, to the best of my knowledge.

REFERENCES

BARRINGER, FELICITY (1999) "Journalism's Greatest Hits", *The New York Times*, 1 March.

BRODIE, FAWN (1974) *Thomas Jefferson: an intimate history*, New York: Norton.

CAMPBELL, W. JOSEPH (2001) *Yellow Journalism: puncturing the myths, defining the legacies*, Westport, CT: Praeger.

CAREY, JAMES (1974) "The Problem of Journalism History", in: *James Carey: a critical reader*, Minneapolis: University of Minnesota Press.

DALY, CHRISTOPHER B. (forthcoming) *Covering America: a narrative history of a nation's journalism*, Amherst, MA: UMass Press.

ELLIS, JOSEPH (1997) *American Sphinx: the character of Thomas Jefferson*, New York: Knopf.

GORDON-REED, ANNETTE (1999 [1997]) *Thomas Jefferson and Sally Hemings: an American controversy*, Charlottesville: University of Virginia Press.

HAMILTON, JOHN MAXWELL (2009) *Journalism's Roving Eye: a history of American foreign reporting*, Baton Rouge, LA: LSU Press.

HAYNES, JOHN EARL and KLEHR, HARVEY (1999) *Venona: decoding Soviet espionage in America*, New Haven: Yale University Press.

HERSEY, JOHN (1946) *Hiroshima*, New York: Knopf.

KNIGHTLEY, PHILLIP (2004 [1975]) *The First Casualty: the war correspondent as hero and myth-maker from the Crimea to Iraq*, Baltimore, MD and London: The Johns Hopkins University Press.

LUBOW, ARTHUR (1992) *The Reporter Who Would Be King: a biography of Richard Harding Davis*, New York: Scribners.

MALONE, DUMAS (1948) *Jefferson and his Time*, Vol. 1, *Jefferson the Virginian*, Charlottesville: University of Virginia Press.

NORD, DAVID PAUL (2001) *Communities of Journalism: a history of American newspapers and their readers*, Urbana and Chicago: University of Illinois Press.

PASLEY, JEFFREY (2001) *The Tyranny of Printers: newspaper politics in the early American republic*, Charlottesville: University of Virginia Press.

REED, JOHN (1919) *Ten Days that Shook the World*, New York: The Modern Library.

SCHUDSON, MICHAEL (1978) *Discovering the News: a social history of American newspapers*, New York: Basic Books.

SHAFER, JACK (2010) "Who Said It First? Journalism is the 'first rough draft of history'", *Slate*, 30 August, http://www.slate.com/id/2265540/pagenum/all/#p2, accessed 22 November 2010.

THOREAU, HENRY DAVID (1991) *Journals*, Vol. 4. Princeton, NJ: Princeton University Press.

WEINGARTEN, MARC (2005) *The Gang that Wouldn't Write Straight: Wolfe, Thompson, Capote and The New Journalism revolution*, New York: Three Rivers Press.

TEACHING JOURNALISM HISTORY TO JOURNALISTS

Andie Tucher

This article is rooted in the experience of helping to develop and introduce a range of required and elective journalism-history courses into a professional school whose jam-packed one-year curriculum has always been dominated by hands-on training in the skills and techniques of the craft. Some of the challenges have been practical and logistical. We decided early on, for instance, that all assignments would involve reading or viewing works of journalism, not secondary sources, but it was harrowing to have to choose no more than three dozen or so pieces to represent three centuries' worth of evolution. And since our limited time required us to focus mainly on journalism history in the United States, we had to decide how elaborately to explain events like the US Civil War that American students had studied from the cradle but that some of our international students could not date within a half-century. But the most interesting, and rewarding, aspect of these courses was watching the changes in the students' thinking about the complexities and conundrums of their chosen profession: the achievements and also the missteps of their predecessors, the contingency of conventions and the mutability of values, the ideas about what journalism is for and how it should be judged. We have not won all of them over yet on the need to spend some of their precious time every week on a course that will not directly contribute to getting them a job. But we do make them think more widely about what that job means. This article charts the institutional and intellectual challenges in constructing a suitable history syllabus at the Columbia Graduate School of Journalism.

Introduction

It is undeniable: students who come to a school of journalism tend to be much more attuned to seconds and minutes than to centuries, much more interested in *today* than in, say, 25 September 1690. That was, of course, the publication date of the first known newspaper in the English-American colonies. But smallpox and ague no longer threaten Boston, New England has given up its invasion of Canada, the lurid rumors about the King of France and his daughter-in-law have died down, and anyway, *Publick Occurrences* is not hiring.

So why on earth would the students at the Columbia Journalism School spend class time reading a 320-year-old rag?

The case can be tough to make. Not only do many students tend to see history in general very much as the character in the 2008 movie *In Bruges* did who dismissed it as "just a load of stuff that's already happened". Not only is the institution of journalism as a whole facing the kind of challenges and pressures—economic disarray, the wild-west uncertainties of the new digital world, the crumbling distinctions between public and professional—that suggest it is the future rather than the past that stands most in need of attention. Not only are there always new skills and techniques to cram into a curriculum already full to bursting. It is also true that journalism history frequently just has not been taught—or studied—very well, that it has too often taken on a triumphalist tone, focusing myopically on the press as an agent of democracy and the public good, and has treated journalistic work as merely an archive of public intelligence or a top-down information system rather than as a dynamically created cultural text (Barnhurst and Nerone, 2009, pp. 24–6; Carey, 1997 [1974]; Collins, 2009).

In the required and elective courses on journalism history that we have added to our curriculum at Columbia over the past decade and more, we have taken a different approach. Journalism, we contend, is both a participant in its culture and a product of it, and to study the history of journalism is at bottom to study the changing ways that societies have told themselves the stories that they recognize as significant and are willing to accept as true to life. Just as the conventions, understandings, values, and expectations that govern fiction have evolved over the years—compare *Clarissa* with, say, *Ulysses*—so too are the particular ways that we tell our truthful stories, even the ways we think about *how* to tell what is truthful, shaped by contingency and context. Our goal is to introduce students to a selection of some of the most important, enlightening, or eloquent journalistic works of the past; press them to recognize and put aside their preconceptions about what journalism now is or ought to be; and lead them to ponder the social relationships, professional assumptions, technological constraints, and cultural contexts that shaped not just the way journalists and their publics created stories together in the past but also the way the students themselves are doing so in the present.

This paper offers some general comments on the state of journalism history in journalism education as well as personal observations on how Columbia's venture has been working.

Journalism History in the Curriculum

Telling journalists what to do has never been simple, but their temperamental and Constitutional resistance to most kinds of regulation seems to have spilled over into any effort to impose order on their education. Just as no one has to go to journalism school in order to become a journalist in the United States, no journalism school has to offer a specific curriculum in order to bestow a journalism degree. The Accrediting Council on Education in Journalism and Mass Communications (ACEJMC) sets standards for degree-granting professional programs and judges their compliance through a process that includes both the institution's own self-study and an independent evaluation by a visiting committee of peers chosen by the council. Undergoing the process is, however, entirely voluntary, and while 112 US programs (and one in Chile) are listed on the council's website (ACEJMC, 2011) as having passed muster, about three-quarters of all the degree-granting programs in the country have chosen not to participate. That apparently does not hurt them; one researcher concludes there is no evidence that accredited schools are "strongly or clearly superior in major ways" to unaccredited schools (Seamon, 2010, pp. 17–18).

Even the schools that choose to undergo the evaluation do not get much direct instruction in *what* they should be teaching. The council "recognizes that each institution has its unique situation, cultural, social or religious context, mission and resources" and thus it "does not define specific curricula, courses or methods of instruction" (ACEJMC, 2004). Among its standards for evaluating curricula is whether students can "demonstrate an understanding of the history and role of professionals and institutions in shaping communications", but the specifics are left entirely unstated. In any case, a survey by the American Journalism Historians Association (AJHA) of schools with graduate mass-communication programs found 52 that reported offering at least one course in history, but another 140 said they offered none (AJHA, 2008).

So the nation's journalism schools have been devising a variety of strategies for accommodating the latest pressures on the profession. Some are envisioning a reorientation of their programs toward the new technologies. The University of Colorado at Boulder, for instance, recently announced that it would be "discontinuing" its School of Journalism and Mass Communications as of 30 June 2011 and terminating its bachelor's degree in journalism. At the same time an exploratory committee was recommending the creation of two new entities, an Institute for the Global Digital Future and a college or school of information, communication, and media technology that would fold the study of journalism into an interdisciplinary program affiliated with film, engineering, business, computer science, law, and other fields. (Also in development is a new dual-major bachelor's degree in journalism and another discipline, which would allow current undergraduates to finish their programs.) Some journalists have been arguing that subsuming journalism into a technologically oriented academic program risked elbowing out instruction in the core skills and values of the craft. But Chancellor Philip P. DiStefano defended the proposed restructuring as "visionary work" that would prepare students for "the new media and networked Information Age environment" (DiStefano quoted in CU-Boulder Office of News Services, 2010; also Brainard, 2011; CU-Boulder Office of the Provost and Executive Vice Chancellor for Academic Affairs, 2011).

Other programs are taking a different perspective on the question of how to prepare journalists for the increasingly complicated task of explaining an increasingly complex world. In 2005, with the support of the Carnegie Foundation and the John S. and James L. Knight Foundation, five research universities—the University of Southern California, the University of California at Berkeley, Harvard, Northwestern, and Columbia—began an initiative on the future of journalism education. Declaring that professional schools ought to function as "the intellectual wing" and the "consciences" of their professions, the five institutions are devoting particular attention to the "enrichment" and "reinvigoration" of the standard journalism curriculum with the stated goal of offering "a deep and multilayered exploration of complex subjects like history, politics, classics and philosophy to undergird their journalistic skills" (Carnegie-Knight Initiative on the Future of Journalism Education, nd a, nd b).

The History of Journalism History at Columbia

As the second-oldest free-standing journalism school in the United States, Columbia had been revamping, revising, and rethinking its curriculum for nearly a century before its involvement in the Carnegie-Knight Initiative, and its emphasis on history and on academic courses in general has waxed and waned and waxed again in that time. When the School first opened its doors in 1912, its main business was, as its founder Joseph Pulitzer had intended, the awarding of a Bachelor of Letters degree to those young men and women who had completed some combination—the precise proportion constantly under adjustment—of practical training and traditional liberal arts courses taken either within or outside the School. But beginning in 1934, when the School reconstituted itself as the first *graduate* journalism school in the United States, the one-year Master of Science curriculum inevitably narrowed. Laboring five days a week in the School's own newsroom, taking mainly required courses in a range of reporting, editing, and production skills, the typical journalism student essentially earned a graduate degree for having survived nine months as a cub reporter.

In the early years the busy curriculum did manage to squeeze in a required course of some kind whose title had something to do with the history of the profession, but its approach was always more utilitarian than conceptual. In the School's annual bulletin for 1935–6, for instance, its first as a graduate institution, the required course in "The History of the Press" was described as devoted to "the development of the modern newspaper with reference to existing conditions and the light they may throw on the theory and practice and journalism in relation to public affairs". And as James Boylan (1988, p. 30) recalled, in the 1950s version of the history class he and his fellow students were assigned "to produce chapter drafts of a group-book (never published) about former Pulitzer Prize winners. Illustrious forbears who had not won Pulitzers, such as Benjamin Franklin, Horace Greeley, or Ida Tarbell, remained unmentioned".

The vast changes in both postwar journalism and the world it covered brought new strains to the jam-packed one-year curriculum. The basic boot-camp-style courses in reporting and writing were constantly being reconfigured, expanding to accommodate broadcasting and splitting into segments to allow students some choice of specialties like cultural affairs or business reporting. The tiny footprint of journalism history in the curriculum, meanwhile, was eroding even more. The 1966–7 bulletin, for instance, listed a one-credit required course in "History and Theory of Communication". Ten years later, the School no longer mandated a history course but it did insist that students choose an elective either from outside the School or from among a short roster of academic-inflected internal offerings that included "History of Journalism" and "The First Amendment". Ten years after that, in 1986–7, the list of electives was both longer and unequivocally practical, and the School offered no full-semester course in journalism history at all.

Over the past 12 years, however, journalism history has been creeping back into the School's curriculum, gaining a larger presence each year. I came to the School in 1998 as the junior professor in Columbia's brand-new Communications PhD program, which had been created by the media scholar James W. Carey and was chaired by him until his death in 2006. The small interdisciplinary program marked the first real departure in more than 60 years from the School's close focus on professional education. Advised by a committee of faculty members from Arts and Sciences, the Business School, and Teachers College as well as the Journalism School, the program allows students to pursue individual plans of study drawing on the graduate resources of the entire university. They have taken classes in everything from Sociology, International Affairs, and Political Science to Architecture, History, and Law in support of their research into such topics as political narrative and "fake news"; mass-mediated terrorism; shifting forms of newswork and cross-institutional journalistic collaboration; a history of Latin American literary journalism; social innovation and wi-fi hotspots; and the subject's experience in the journalistic interview.

My own background as a journalist, a historian, and the author of a book about the nineteenth-century origins of the urban mass press in the United States inspired me to develop as my first offering a survey course in the history of American journalism that I expected would be of interest mainly to our PhDs. I was both surprised and pleased, however, to find that each year at least half a dozen or so of our MS students chose to take it as their spring elective instead of more career-oriented alternatives such as computer-assisted reporting or sportswriting. (Their motives, I allow, were mixed. While many said they had become interested in the topic because of the two 90-minute lectures surveying the profession's history that I always presented during the August orientation period, or were happy for the chance to take something that "felt more like the kind of college classes I'm used to", some clearly relished the respite that my reading-centered course gave them from yet another subway ride to nethermost Queens or the back of the Bronx for yet more shoeleather reporting.) Just as gratifying was the interest of students from other parts of the university: over the years I have had at least one person from almost every division at Columbia, from the undergraduate colleges to the medical school. While some were pursuing specific research plans in aspects of communications history, most said they were simply interested in journalism and eager to explore how it worked.

Teaching a class whose students brought so wide a range of backgrounds, interests, preparations, and goals was often challenging, but the range of their experience could often add an unexpected pungency to the discussion. For the first class, for instance, I assigned students to browse through the single known issue of that pioneering sheet *Publick Occurrences*, the full text of which is available online.[1] Among the secondary readings assigned, which were required only for the PhD students but "warmly recommended" for everyone else, was David Paul Nord's incisive article (1990) arguing that the roots of the modern news system were planted in the intensely theocratic culture of seventeenth-century New England long before the appearance of anything that looked like a modern newspaper. The empirical accounts of miracles, comets, and monstrous births that appeared so often in pamphlets, ballads, printed sermons, and almanacs, Nord suggested, were in fact *news*, conveying important current public information about the most essential possible object of attention: God's plan for humankind.

So the students who read Nord's piece came to class well primed to lead a conversation about why editor Ben Harris described as the *first* of his three goals the dissemination of "Memorable Occurrents of Divine Providence", or about the close attention his paper gave to the suicide of a recent widower of whose "Melancholly" the "Devil took advantage". The entire class was prepared to debate the contingency of what the definition of *news* was and who had the power to define and direct it. But then an MS student immersed in the importance of the Five W's raised an intriguing set of questions that her more academically inclined classmates had not considered. Why did the Devil have a name in the suicide story when the dead widower did not? What does that suggest about another of Harris's goals, to use "the best fountains for our information" to ensure that everything he printed was true? Why would an element that we have come to regard as the "first W" have been seen as unimportant or unnecessary? What is a "fact", anyway, how do readers use facts to judge the credibility of a story, and what is the relationship between fact and truth? That 320-year-old rag clearly maintains the power to inform the thinking of the 10-times-great-grandchildren of editor Ben Harris.

For several years, my elective was the only formal offering in history in a busy curriculum that remained largely practical. In 2002 the coincident arrival of Lee C. Bollinger as Columbia's new president and the School's search for a new dean offered a wide-open opportunity to review and rethink not just our own curriculum but also the state of journalism education as a whole. President Bollinger, a legal scholar with a particular interest in the First Amendment, convened a task force that included both working journalists and faculty members from the School, the larger university, and beyond. Their mandate was to explore the question of "how journalism education in a great university can contribute to the process by which the media adapt to a new world", as President Bollinger wrote in a statement on the future of journalism (2003). The chair of the task force was Nicholas Lemann, the author of five books on history and current affairs who had also served on the staffs of *The New Yorker*, the *Washington Post*, and other prominent publications.

The report that Lemann wrote summing up the deliberations of the task force stressed the special responsibilities, opportunities, and challenges afforded by the School's unique position (Lemann, 2003). Nearly all of the degree-granting journalism programs in the United States are based at public universities, whose traditional mission of emphasizing utilitarian and vocational instruction has continued to encourage the view of journalism as one more kind of practical trade. Columbia, on the other hand, as a major private research university, is in a position to conduct all of its professional schools including Journalism "in a manner consistent with its overall commitment to honoring intellectual life", Lemann wrote (2003), "and to maintaining a critical distance from the field in which its graduates will be employed". A professional school within a private research university can embrace some of the goals that pervade the larger institution, Lemann continued, among them to offer curricula that "try to teach their students 'how to think', in ways that are distinctive to the profession and that will be useful for many years, rather than simply teaching them entry-level job skills", and to "try to place the profession in a larger context that will enable students not to be imprisoned by its automatic assumptions, and, institutionally, to be an improving force within their professions". Upon the disbanding of the task force, in 2003, Lemann was named Dean of the School.

Columbia's Changing Curriculum

Changes soon began percolating through the curriculum. In 2005–6, with the help of a Carnegie-Knight grant, the School launched a new Master of Arts degree in Journalism that forges an intellectual link between the School and Columbia's faculty of arts and science. The program, open to MS graduates and working journalists with commensurate skills, in effect turns general-assignment reporters into skilled specialists in one of four topics of public interest and importance: science and the environment; arts and culture; business and economics; and politics. Each student takes a year-long seminar in his or her major, co-taught by journalists from our faculty and academics from other departments, that combines intensive journalistic work with immersion in the intellectual substance of the field. Also required are two new Journalism courses designed especially for this program: "Evidence & Inference", conducted by Dean Lemann and others, which teaches advanced research skills geared for news professionals, and "History of Journalism for Journalists".

Intended as it is for students who are both professionally experienced and academically ambitious, the MA History course takes an expansive and thematic approach to exploring the basic question of how the organized human activity of journalism works and how it has varied over time and across national traditions. The course has been taught for the past five years by Michael Schudson, a sociologist who has written often about historical matters and who has a knack for raising provocative questions. The syllabus lists the topic for the fourth week, for instance, as "Does Jefferson Belong on His Pedestal? If

There Was a First Amendment in 1791, Why Was There a Sedition Act in 1798?" In other weeks the class examines Tocqueville's European vision of the "strange Americans", takes an excerpt from Walter Lippmann's *Liberty and the News* as the basis for asking "Does Democracy Need Journalism—If So, What Kind?", and wades fearlessly into the debate over "Entertainment, Vulgarity, and Democracy: Is Vulgarity Bad for Us?" While the focus of the course remains on US practice, Schudson's 2010 syllabus reflected the students' expressed interest in a more international approach by incorporating aspects of media development in France, Japan, India, the Netherlands, and Sweden.

The MS requirements were the next to come under scrutiny. For many years the School had introduced students to the standards and traditions of the profession through two all-class foundation courses. On Friday mornings most of the students gathered for "Journalism, the Law, and Society", taught by two legal scholars who discussed key court cases in press law and such fundamental First Amendment issues as libel, prior restraint, and the protection of sources. (A separate section provided international students with a more intensive introduction to US politics and society.) The afternoon was devoted to "Critical Issues in Journalism", team-taught in Socratic style by Prof. Carey and Prof. Stephen Isaacs, who pressed the students to ponder a range of ethical and practical issues: What does "independent" journalism mean? What qualifies as "news"? Can a journalist be both truthful and humane? Some of the topics necessarily drew on historical examples, but the emphasis was on present-day dilemmas.

A growing sense among faculty members that those courses were not keeping up with the twenty-first-century media landscape led to a radical reconfiguration of not just the content but also the structure of the old courses. In 2009–10 the School launched its new requirement, a four-credit package that we are calling "Journalism Essentials" and that consists of four mini-courses of half a semester each. Each mini-course is offered four times; in random order each student takes two during the first half of the semester and the other two in the second half. Three of the four new courses will surprise no one: "Business of Journalism" covers both institutional and newer stand-alone models for the business of gathering and publishing the news; "Ethics of Journalism" relies heavily on in-depth case studies of contemporary professional dilemmas; and "Law of Journalism" addresses the practical legal issues that reporters are likely to face whether they are working for an organization or on their own. The fourth was the first *required* course in journalism history for MS students that anyone here can remember.

The goals are simple. As Dean Lemann summed up in a recent conversation with me: "we want to give students both a *canon* and a *context*"—to acquaint them with some of the great works of journalism but also to make clear the relationships between journalism and the contemporary stream of activity that produced it. We hope that students will thus be inspired to think broadly about the origins, purposes, and effects of the conventions they themselves follow, or at least to understand that they are not the first journalists in the world to think of *this* or worry about *that*. (As Lemann put it, "they should know that we've fallen off the cliff before.")

The challenges, however, are plenty. That very word "required", of course, automatically casts an "eat your spinach" aura over a course that many students were instinctively viewing with attitudes ranging from indifference to alarm, but it comes with added complications. The course is big; with between 60 and 70 students in each section, it is too unwieldy to work as a discussion-centered course. It is short; deciding what to cover and, worse, what to leave out in our seven two-and-a-half-hour meetings requires hard-nosed choices. It has a wildly diverse student body; in 2009–10, our inaugural year, nearly one-third of the 263 full-time students hailed from outside the United States and reported 31 countries of origin ranging from Canada to Ethiopia and the United Arab Emirates. And to top it all off, it meets on Fridays, the end of a long, busy week that generally involves students in constant reporting trips by bus, subway, or foot.

To put together the syllabus I worked with Dean Lemann, himself a historian, who in the first year taught one of the four sections. We decided early on that for so varied a group with only a modest store of common knowledge and without much experience in the conventions of historical research and scholarship, direct encounters with works of historical journalism would be more enlightening and engaging than would assignments in secondary sources. And although we wanted to make sure that the students read some of the best examples of their predecessors' work, canons can, of course, be misleading. In compiling our reading list, we were determined to avoid the too-common response of reveling in the profession's heroic mode—the First Amendment, World War II, the Pentagon Papers, Watergate—but quietly eliding the many misjudgments and gaffes that mottle its record. Yes, ambitious young correspondents might well find their own inspiration in the cunning of Martha Gellhorn, who talked her way aboard a hospital ship on D-Day, turned in to *Collier's* a harrowing yet eloquent account of the carnage on Omaha Beach, and in the process scooped her hypercompetitive husband, Ernest Hemingway, who never actually made it ashore. Weary young metro reporters might well find the strength to dial one more number or knock on one more door by recalling the doggedness of Woodward and Bernstein, who refused to accept the common wisdom that the break-in at the Watergate office building was no more than a third-rate burglary. But aspiring journalists should also benefit from the cautionary examples of the scabrous partisanship of the 1790s, the lurid excesses of the yellow press, the faintheartedness of the McCarthy era, or that time when the Watergate reporters' *too* dogged pursuit of grand-jury testimony earned them a rebuke from a federal judge.

And we made the difficult decision to focus mainly on US journalism. Logistical justifications were powerful: with just seven sessions at our disposal, any attempt to cover the entire world would reduce us to a dreary and uninformative recitation of bullet points, and since we are basing the course on primary sources everyone is presumed to have read, our only common language is English. But our decision was rooted in good intellectual reasons as well. Most of the students come to the School to learn to be the particular kind of journalist known as the reporter, and it was the United States that essentially invented that job description beginning in the 1830s, when the rise to dominance of the mass commercial press established many of the traditions, standards, and rules that reporters nowadays either follow or decide to transgress.

We organized the seven-week curriculum in a generally chronological order but defined and explored each era thematically according to the most distinctive develop-ments in the ways that journalistic work was conceived, viewed, and carried out at the time. The chronological boundaries were loose; we felt free to root or follow a given theme forwards or backwards in time in an intellectually coherent way rather than marching straight ahead through the decades. An overview of the Fall 2010 syllabus is given in Appendix A.

It was, of course, painful to choose the small handful of pieces that would represent three centuries' worth of evolution across the spectrum of media and genres from the alternative paper to the evening news broadcast, from the daguerreotype to the blog, from the investigative unit to the sports page. In the end, we fudged our numbers a little, generally listing only four or five items as required for all but adding half dozen or more "recommended readings" each week. The final exam asks students to choose and analyze some of those.

Also challenging was our own commitment to do justice to diversity while still acknowledging the reality that for a large part of its life, US journalism, like so many western historical institutions, was dominated by white men. Determined not to follow the common practice of ghettoizing works by women or people of color into a single unit under some deprecatory rubric like "other voices", we sought whenever we could to move beyond the usual suspects and draw our assignments from a wide variety of writers. We did, indeed, devote a week to the particular character of journalism produced by and for self-identified communities or publics, but among the examples of that journalism we included the US Army's newspaper *Stars and Stripes* along with the NAACP's *Crisis* magazine, the conservative commentator William F. Buckley along with the feminist Susan Brownmiller.

Into every week's topic we integrated a range of voices. The Civil War reporter Thomas Morris Chester of the *Philadelphia Press*, for instance, was typical of the war correspondent of the era in every way save one: he was a free black man. Our week on the traditionally aggressive and "male" art of investigative reporting could not and did not ignore either Woodward and Bernstein on Watergate or Seymour Hersh on the My Lai massacre. But it also easily accommodated an excerpt from *Silent Spring*, Rachel Carson's long 1962 exposé of the damages caused by the overuse of chemical pesticides, and Vera Connolly's "Cry of a Broken People", about oppressive conditions on Native American reservations, that had been published in 1929 in (of all places) the quintessential women's magazine *Good Housekeeping*.

We did not always get it right. Our first syllabus included a selection from Addison and Steele's *Spectator*, for instance, but my attempt to introduce the idea of the "public" through a description of classic coffeehouse culture left too many students wondering what the art of the elegant essay had to do with Starbucks. Many of them simply did not get Alexis de Tocqueville; many found Ida Tarbell tedious (well, so do I) or Norman Mailer bombastic (ditto). And since journalism is so often written for the moment, some of the most interesting practitioners—H. L. Mencken and I. F. Stone among them—can be a chore for readers lodged in their own and much later moments to comprehend.

We saw as one of our paramount tasks the opening of their historical imaginations, but that meant more than just pressing them to test their assumptions; for many students the greater challenges lay in recognizing that they even *had* assumptions in the first place and in accepting that the present was not automatically better than the past. So for the first class meeting, I chose pieces that smelled like news accounts but directly challenged the conventions and understandings that most of us bring to our engagement with present-day journalism. We discussed how Christopher Columbus established (or abused) his credibility in his widely published and un-fact-checkable letter about his voyage to the New World, considered the presence of the divine in *Publick Occurrences*, and pondered the placement of Blackbeard's head.[2] That came in the story from the *Boston News-Letter* for 23 February/2 March 1719 about the great sea battle between the royal navy and the "Notorious and Arch Pirate Capt. Teach". The relatively long article slowly unfolded a thrilling narrative: the scene was set, the enemy sighted, the frantic combat described blow by blow, and, finally, the pirate beheaded. At first the students snickered knowingly about the buried lede, and when asked how they themselves would write the story for tomorrow's *New York Times*, effortlessly served up the kind of first sentence any editor nowadays would love: "Holding aloft the severed head of the pirate Blackbeard, Lieutenant Robert Maynard of *H.M.S. Pearl* returned home today..." But we eventually worked our way around to a very different view of the question. Given, on the one hand, a story with a beginning, a middle, and a particularly rousing end, and on the other, an account that divorces cause from effect, warps chronology, and steps on the punchline, which is really the weirder narrative strategy, and what purpose does it serve?

An even greater challenge to their assumptions was the unsigned article in the *Boston Gazette* of 12 March 1770 describing the "Boston Massacre", the violent confrontation between British troops and rebellious citizens that helped edge the colonies closer to their revolution. The article popped with outrage as it described how a small group of Redcoats armed with cutlasses, muskets, and clubs began chasing and assaulting unarmed citizens in the streets. When the Bostonians responded by lobbing snowballs, the soldiers opened fire and dropped a number of men into the snow. "But what shewed a degree of cruelty ... was an attempt to fire upon or push with their bayonets the persons who undertook to remove the slain and wounded!" The descriptions of the victims' injuries were explicit: Crispus Attucks had been gored in the lung and "most horribly" in the liver; a ball had carried off a chunk of Samuel Gray's skull; and a widow's son, "a promising youth of 17 years of age", had taken a ball in the belly and died after it was "cut out at his back".

The students were skeptical of the story, and proud of their skepticism. They were not surprised to learn that the Bostonians had actually been taunting the Redcoats with weapons much less benign than snowballs; some of them even knew that the death toll of the "massacre" was five. So when I asked them to describe what the newspaper had been up to, the answer was swift: it was bias, pure and simple. The newspaper was violating every tenet of objective reporting.

What makes you expect, I asked them, that the newspaper *should* have been objective?

Well, they said, in those days reporters were not as professional; they let their bias show. Clear in the students' answer was the subtext: *we* would not have been so primitive.

Again I asked: what makes you expect that the newspaper should *not* have been biased?

They grew a little restive—hadn't they answered that already? Well, they ventured, in wartime readers do not *want* a newspaper to be balanced, they *want* propaganda. Subtext: a really responsible journalist would not have given it to them.

I asked my question again: what makes you expect that the newspaper *should* have been balanced? It took several more tries before one of them grasped the point that maybe the *Gazette* was not actually "violating" any rules of objectivity; maybe there were no such rules at the time to violate. Some seemed shocked to learn that for the first half-century of its life, the new nation intended and expected its newspapers to take a direct role in shaping political opinion and fostering political debate, the tone of which could range from hearty to over-excited to vile. But as we went on to explore the proposition that the very words they had been using—biased, unbalanced, not objective—embodied concepts that no reader or editor of the time would have recognized, they began to toy with the radical notion that since the ideal of objectivity had not, in fact, been handed down to journalists on a stone tablet in the mists of the past, maybe it could stand some reappraisal in the present.

A key element of the course was performance: teaching a Friday-afternoon lecture class in a topic that many students *expected* to find boring inspired me to discover and liberate my inner ham. Plentiful props and visual materials also helped keep things lively. My collection of real and facsimile newspapers from various eras helped students visualize the changes in the work that produced those pages, and their answers to my standard question "What do you *not* see"? evolved over the weeks: illustrations, then photographs; headlines, then decked headlines; display ads, then front-page ads. To the first class I brought a purchase from the local toy store: the foot-high G.I. Joe action figure fully equipped with a tiny newspaper, a miniature typewriter, and dog tags identifying him as "Ernie Pyle", the beloved reporter who covered World War II one ordinary soldier at a time. Proof positive, I said, that sometimes the public actually *likes* journalists. I am not sure, however, that I will add the new "TV News Anchor Barbie" doll, complete with microphone, camera, and tight pink ruffled miniskirt, to my collection.

Some of the two dozen or so slides I projected each week from my computer were simply photographs, video clips, or excerpts from the pieces under discussion, but other slides were designed to inveigle, unsettle, or startle the students into engaging with the historical context. Discussing the birth of the reporter in the nineteenth century, for instance, I wanted to make a larger point about how different in general were nineteenth-century assumptions about education, vocational preparation, and the very idea of a "profession". So I displayed an excerpt from the popular medical handbook *Gunn's Domestic Medicine and Poor Man's Friend*, first published in 1830, which assured the reader that if he had a large carving knife, some strips of linen, and enough helpers to hold the patient down, "any man, unless he be an idiot or an absolute fool", could amputate a limb.

The class was too large for intimate discussion, but I often lobbed juicy questions at them (Did Walker Evans's photographs of poor sharecropper families exploit his subjects? Do you agree with the *New York Times*'s decision to soften the Bay of Pigs story when the Kennedy Administration invoked "national security"? Do you trust Truman Capote?), and encouraged anyone with a question or comment to speak up. And to make sure everyone opened his or her mouth at least once, each student was expected to prepare a brief commentary of three to five minutes about "something you find interesting, puzzling, provoking, or weird" in one of the required or recommended readings and present it to his or her classmates. That meant that each week eight or ten different students would be speaking in class about something that intrigued them.

Each class meeting had its moments of contention, surprise, and illumination. But one of the most memorable exchanges came when I least expected it: in response to a story I had assigned from the 15 April 1971 issue of the alternative weekly *Village Voice* called "On Goosing".

It was for the session on "Journalists and Their Publics" that we read Susan Brownmiller's droll yet pointed account of her impulsive retaliation against a stranger who made an offensive sexual advance. Mindful that English was a second language for many class members, I started by asking "Do you all understand what goosing is?" But the rows of blank looks I got quickly made clear that even some of the students raised on American slang were unfamiliar with the term.

"It's like pinching, right?", ventured one.

Well, sometimes, I said, but it often refers to something rougher, as in this case: the aggressive groping of a woman's crotch in public by a man she didn't know.

As several of the young women gasped audibly, one blurted: "Why on earth would anyone want to do that?"

I couldn't help it. "I can't tell you how happy I am that all this is news to you," I said. "I'm younger than Brownmiller, but in the seventies my female friends and I just accepted that when you were out in the street you might be goosed at any time. We all were. This is one giant leap for humankind!"

That broke the ice for a zingy class discussion. One of the students who had been assigned to comment on the piece said that Brownmiller had undermined her credibility by quoting the "extreme" feminist argument that rape was a metaphor for all male–female relationships. Other students leapt into the fray to defend or criticize. Then one pointed out that Brownmiller's essay had appeared just a few years after Valerie Solanas shot Andy Warhol and wrote her "SCUM Manifesto" advocating the destruction of the male sex, "which just goes to show", he said, "that feminists really *were* extreme". Injecting some good old objective balance, I pointed out that many women, then as now, rejected feminism—the most effective opponent of the Equal Rights Amendment to the Constitution was Phyllis Schlafly—but that most feminists rejected Solanas, too. As for the rape metaphor, I said, evaluate it in its historical and legal context: until state laws began to change in the late seventies, a man was generally exempt from prosecution for sexual assault or abuse if the victim in question was his wife.

Some jaws dropped. Some clenched.

The conversation gradually turned to some of the questions I had had in mind when I chose Brownmiller's work for assignment. What does advocacy journalism do that objective journalism cannot? Whom was this journalist writing for? What kind of relationship does advocacy journalism build with its readers and how is it different from what objective journalism does? Someone pointed out how surprising it was to find a piece of unabashedly opinionated journalism that was also funny. Yes, said someone else, it's especially refreshing to find a funny feminist given their reputation for humorlessness. A piece they had read earlier by W. E. B. Du Bois, she went on, was an important and passionate argument on behalf of civil rights for African Americans, but it was also so grim and accusatory that she could not imagine that anyone who did not already agree with Du Bois would want to read it. Brownmiller's sprightly style could be inviting even to people who were not necessarily feminists—or women, either.

But the conversation pushed into territory that was new even to me when a young woman in the back of the room asked, hesitantly, whether I would mind talking about how I had felt when I was goosed. Did I fight back? Did I report it? Nonplused at finding myself on the other end of the questioning, I tried to answer honestly. I had felt angry and demeaned but in no way seriously damaged, and no, I had done nothing about it; it had never occurred to me that I could protest.

"Then Brownmiller was writing for you. *You* should have been reading the *Village Voice!*", she said.

That conversation realized many of the hopes I had had for the course. The students were using a journalistic work that happened to be from the past in exactly the ways most people initially use journalism: to encounter new information or points of view, to challenge and shape their own thinking, to launch a debate with others. But they were also evaluating the way the piece worked *as* journalism, drawing conclusions about tone and style that they could bring to their own work and analyzing the various ways that other readers might use the journalism for themselves. They were, in short, understanding journalism as a social instrument, as both a participant in its culture and a product of it.

The course, about to enter its third year, is still evolving. The students have voiced criticisms; some have told us they wish we spent more time on international topics or that the group were smaller to make conversation easier. Some still grumble about squandering precious time and energy on a subject that will not teach them a skill or get them a job. Many, however, have come to the same conclusion and expressed it with the same sense of surprise. They never thought, they said, that history could be either interesting or informative. But even journalists can find value in things that did not happen *today*.

NOTES

1. See http://en.wikisource.org/wiki/Publick_Occurrences_Both_Forreign_and_Domestick.
2. Clark (1994, pp. 218–19) makes a similar point using a much shorter version of the Blackbeard story that ran in the previous issue of the *News-Letter*.

REFERENCES

ACCREDITING COUNCIL ON EDUCATION IN JOURNALISM AND MASS COMMUNICATIONS (ACEJMC) (2004) "ACEJMC Accrediting Standards", http://www2.ku.edu/~acejmc/PROGRAM/STANDARDS.SHTML, accessed 13 May 2011.

ACCREDITING COUNCIL ON EDUCATION IN JOURNALISM AND MASS COMMUNICATIONS (ACEJMC) (2011) "ACEJMC Accredited Programs 2010–2011", updated 15 March, http://www2.ku.edu/~acejmc/STUDENT/PROGLIST.SHTML, accessed 13 May 2011.

AMERICAN JOURNALISM HISTORIANS ASSOCIATION (AJHA) (2008) *Report of the Graduate Subcommittee of the AJHA Task Force on History in the Curriculum*, David Sloan, chair, 25 August, http://ajhaonline.org/document_downloads/gradsubcommittee.pdf, accessed 13 May 2011.

BARNHURST, KEVIN G. and NERONE, JOHN (2009) "Journalism History", in: Karin Wahl-Jorgensen and Thomas Hanitzsch (Eds), *The Handbook of Journalism Studies*, New York and London: Routledge, pp. 17–28.

BOLLINGER, LEE C. (2003) "Columbia News: President Bollinger's statement on the future of journalism education", Columbia University Office of Public Affairs, modified 18 April, http://www.columbia.edu/cu/news/03/04/lcb_j_task_force.html, accessed 13 May 2011.

BOYLAN, JAMES (1988) "Declarations of Independence", *Columbia Journalism Review*, November/December, pp. 29–45.

BRAINARD, CURTIS (2011) "CU-Boulder to Shutter J-school", *The Observatory: Columbia Journalism Review*, 19 April, http://www.cjr.org/the_observatory/cu-boulder_to_shutter_j-school.php, accessed 13 May 2011.

CAREY, JAMES W. (1997 [1974]) "The Problem of Journalism History", in: Eve Stryker Munson and Catherine A. Warren (Eds), *James Carey: a critical reader*, Minneapolis and London: University of Minnesota Press, pp. 86–94.

CARNEGIE-KNIGHT INITIATIVE ON THE FUTURE OF JOURNALISM EDUCATION (nd a) "Curriculum Enrichment", http://newsinitiative.org/initiative/curriculum.html, accessed 13 May 2011.

CARNEGIE-KNIGHT INITIATIVE ON THE FUTURE OF JOURNALISM EDUCATION (nd b) "A Manifesto", http://newsinitiative.org/taskforce/manifesto.html, accessed 13 May 2011.

CLARK, CHARLES E. (1994) *The Public Prints: the newspaper in Anglo-American culture, 1665–1740*, New York and Oxford: Oxford University Press.

COLLINS, ROSS F. (2009) "Towards a Definition of Journalism History", *American Journalism* 26(1), pp. 175–6.

CU-BOULDER OFFICE OF NEWS SERVICES (2010) "CU-Boulder Committee to Study Future of Journalism Course and Degree Offerings", 25 August, http://www.colorado.edu/news/r/9633a0d50 68731edbbd4a81eb12cb101.html, accessed 13 May 2011.

CU-BOULDER OFFICE OF THE PROVOST AND EXECUTIVE VICE CHANCELLOR FOR ACADEMIC AFFAIRS (2011) "Acceptance of the ICT Exploratory Committee Report", 14 February, http://academic affairs.colorado.edu/academicreview/wordpress/wp-content/uploads/2011/02/Final-ICT-Reportw_Provost-Acceptance.pdf, accessed 13 May 2011.

LEMANN, NICHOLAS B. (2003) "A Two-year Journalism School Curriculum: report to the Bollinger task force, Columbia University Graduate School of Journalism", February.

NORD, DAVID PAUL (1990) "Teleology and News: the religious roots of American journalism, 1630–1730", *Journal of American History* 77, pp. 9–38.

SEAMON, MARK C. (2010) "The Value of Accreditation: an overview of three decades of research comparing accredited and unaccredited journalism and mass communications programs", *Journalism & Mass Communication Educator* 65(1), pp. 10–20.

Appendix A

Fall 2010 Syllabus

Week 1: Journalism Before Reporters.   Regularly printed sheets containing current information were being produced in Europe by the early seventeenth century, but general assumptions about the content, purpose, and readership of these new-fangled newspapers were very different from those now taught in J-school.

Readings included: Christopher Columbus; *Publick Occurrences*; Thomas Paine; the *Boston Gazette* on the massacre; Marat on the execution of Louis XVI; partisan papers of the 1790s.

Week 2: The Emergence of the Reporter.   The independent, entrepreneurial reporter is born, and we'll be exploring how he or she went about defining the job.

Readings included: Edgar Allen Poe and Walt Whitman; Civil War reporting; Mark Twain in the *Territorial Enterprise*; Nellie Bly's undercover investigation of an insane asylum; Richard Harding Davis in Cuba.

Week 3: Reporters and their Publics.   Reporters have always served many different publics and forged many different kinds of relationships with their readers/viewers. Here we consider the nature of the reporter's role toward self-identified publics and explore the deep roots and long appeal of opinion journalism.

Readings included: opinion pieces by W. E. B. Du Bois, H. L. Mencken, William F. Buckley, and Kathleen Parker; T. Thomas Fortune in the *New York Globe*; Sgt. Alexander Woollcott in *Stars and Stripes*; Brownmiller's "On Goosing".

Week 4: Reporters and Their Tools.   Every generation of reporters is faced with its own new technologies, but questions about the things each new technology can and can't do are always accompanied by other, often harder ones: what are the things each new technology should and should not do?

Readings (and clips) included: the Associated Press following the assassination of Abraham Lincoln; Edison films, both authentic and staged, on the Spanish–American War; photographs by Jacob Riis and Walker Evans; radio and television reporting by Edward R. Murrow; World War II newsreels.

Week 5: Reporters and the Powers That Be.   The press in the United States has always been expected to serve as a watchdog on those in power, a duty recognized in the first amendment to the Constitution and resoundingly upheld two centuries later in the Pentagon Papers case. Yet while many journalists have assumed the watchdog function, others have acted more like lap dogs or even hot dogs.

Readings included: muckraking by Samuel Hopkins Adams; Vera Connolly; *I.F. Stone's Weekly*; Rachel Carson; Seymour Hersh; Woodward and Bernstein; civil rights coverage by Harrison Salisbury and John Herbers; the *Wall Street Journal* investigates President Lyndon Johnson's wealth; CBS's Morley Safer in Vietnam.

Week 6: Reporters and the New Journalisms.   Reporters are constantly reinventing, rethinking, and reworking the rules, expectations, and traditions of journalism; there have been many "New Journalisms". What do they accomplish that "old-fashioned" journalism doesn't? Do they do anything they shouldn't?

Readings included: A. J. Liebling, John Steinbeck, Martha Gellhorn, Joan Didion, Gay Talese, Truman Capote, Hunter Thompson, Susan Orlean, Isabel Wilkerson, Tom Wolfe.

Week 7: Journalism After Reporters?   Just as the telegraph and the radio did, just as Benjamin Franklin Bache and Tom Wolfe did, the Internet is changing journalism yet again, and the job of the reporter along with it. What's next?

Readings included: citizen journalism on Huffingtonpost.com; crowd-sourcing on Talkingpointsmemo.com; criticism of the mainstream media on LittleGreenFootballs.com; live-blogging of protest and tragedy; Yoani Sanchez's bilingual blog from Cuba.

BROADSHEETS, BROADCASTS AND BOTANY BAY
History in the Australian media

Bridget Griffen-Foley

The "Australians and the Past" survey in the late 1990s showed that the vast majority of people gained their principal historical understanding from some form of entertainment across their lifetime. For over a century the media has been a key source in the development of Australians' historical understanding and historical consciousness. This article explores some of the many ways history has been presented by Australian journalists and other media practitioners, focusing on the press and radio, since World War I. The article surveys the coverage of the 1938 sesquicentenary of the British settlement of Australia, history pages in Australian newspapers, and an unusual historical newspaper published in 1948–9. It traces how the emergence of the Australian Broadcasting Commission and commercial radio during the interwar years created a new outlet for popular historians led by Frank Clune and distinguished professors such as S. H. Roberts. In doing so, it considers the role of journalism, and the media more generally, in creating a national narrative around Anzac Day; recognising indigenous dispossession; and facilitating the emergence of Australian public historians and intellectuals.

Introduction

The "Australians and the Past" survey of historical consciousness in the late 1990s showed that the vast majority of Australians gained their principal historical under- standing from some form of entertainment across their lifetime. One of the most common activities—for 84.2 per cent of respondents—was watching historical movies or documentaries on television. The "media", including newspapers and radio programs, was recorded as a source for history, and the survey suggested that newspaper articles and scrapbooks were collected by people who were researching history (Hamilton and Ashton, 2003, pp. 11, 13, 15–16, 26).

As Kevin Williams (2008, p. 12) notes in relation to Britain, there was a vogue for all things historical in the 1840s and 1850s, a period during which the academic teaching of the subject was relatively unimportant. In Australia, historical features have been appearing in the Australian press since at least the 1850s. Journalists have written local histories, state histories and biographies, as Prue Torney-Parlicki (1999) showed in an important piece on the Australian journalist as historian. In the nineteenth century, Australian journalists formed the largest occupational group who wrote history (see also Dickenson, 2010). Journalists, often as foreign and war correspondents,[1] have authored contemporaneous histories, ranging from William Coote and George Sutherland in the nineteenth century (Cryle, 1990; Morrison, 1969; Sutherland 1880; Sutherland and Sutherland, 1877) to M. H. Ellis (1949), Alan Reid (1971, 1976) and Paul Kelly (1994,

2009) in the twentieth and twenty-first centuries. Several, including Betty Osborn in Victoria (Lemon, 2008), Clem Lack in Queensland (Kerr, 2000), Ivor Birtwistle in Western Australia (Porter, 1993), and Frank Bladen (Fletcher, 2005), Arthur Jose (Lamont, 1983) and George Mackaness (Mitchell and Rutledge, 1986) with the Royal Australian Historical Society, played key roles in the establishment and leadership of historical societies.

This article considers some of the many ways in which history has been presented by the Australian media since the 1920s. Its focus is wider than "journalism". The article begins with a journalist during World War I, but ends with the Social History Unit of the Australian Broadcasting Commission (ABC). It includes a brief discussion of Frank Clune, who was unquestionably the most popular Australian historian of the mid-twentieth century and a multi-media personality, even though he was not a journalist himself (Griffen-Foley, 2011). The article moves between special and regular history pages in the Australian press, an unusual historical newspaper published in 1948–9, public broadcasting (the ABC) and commercial radio. It concentrates on non-fiction, with television historical drama and film beyond the scope of this article.

World War I might be thought of as something of a turning point for the media's role in shaping a national and/or historical consciousness in Australia. A young Australian journalist, Keith Murdoch, wrote a sensational letter condemning the "deplorable" bungling of the British army and lauding the "magnificent manhood" of Australian troops at Anzac Cove in April 1915; the letter contributed to General Sir Ian Hamilton's recall and the evacuation of troops (Murdoch, 2010; *Sydney Morning Herald*, 1968a, 1968b, 1968c, 1968d, 1968e; Younger, 2003; Zwar, 1980).[2] C. E. W. Bean, who had narrowly defeated Murdoch in an Australian Journalists' Association ballot to become the official Australian war correspondent, did most to create and maintain the Anzac legend in his journalism and books from 1915 onwards (Williams, 1999). In June 1915 the Victorian journalist Ernest Buley wrote *The Dardenelles: their story and their significance in the Great War*, hailed as "the first Anzac book"; he followed it with *A Child's History of Anzac* in 1916 (Lack, 2005). As Williams (2008, p. 11) observes, the media are and always have been intimately tied up with the construction of national identities, and popular national myths and legends.

History on Radio

Some, albeit not sustained, scholarly attention has been given to the intersections between Australian journalism and the press, and the Anzac legend in particular and history in general. There has been no equivalent study of the role of public broadcasting in recording and making history, and commercial radio has been, until recently (Griffen-Foley, 2009), a sector even more neglected by Australian historians.

Applying for a broadcasting licence in 1926 for what became Sydney's 2GB, A. E. Bennett from the Theosophical Society wrote: "The intention is to conduct the station on ideal principles and solely with the object of uplifting our Australian people". Amidst classical music and lectures of "high standing" would be talks "on the great men of history ... with the Object of developing in our Australian Nation a high culture similar to that of the older countries of the world but with our purely national characteristics".[3] Exemplary figures from the past were to become frequent subjects of talks on the new medium of radio (Macintyre, 1994, p. 36). Biographical subjects were generally classical, British or European, and targeted more at male interests.

When, in 1934, a new 2GB announcer, John Creighton, began presenting "topical and historic" sketches, under the general title of *Glimpses of the Great*, he explained that they would be broadcast at 3.45 pm weekdays, "the time when most women are taking a rest" (*Wireless Weekly*, 1934a). Later, other commercial stations included in their daytime programming aimed at women talks on female historical figures. 2UW was presenting a *Women in History* series by 1945. A sample from March shows talks on Queen Zenobia; the Duchess of Gordon; Elizabeth Farren, an eighteenth-century actress; and Nino de Lenclos, a French beauty (*Radio Pictorial of Australia*, 1945).

Australian history—occasionally even touching on indigenous history—gradually made its way on to the airwaves. In 1928 a Presbyterian minister, William Robertson, broadcasting as "Brin-ga", presented lectures on Sydney's 2BL (later part of the ABC) about Aborigines and his own experiences living with them over the past 50 years. Robertson relayed his stories by means of the "long coo-ee" (the wireless), and published the substantial series as *Coo-ee Talks*, with an introduction by the anthropologist Herbert Basedow (Robertson, 1928).[4]

There were other broadcasts that touched on the issues of race and gender in Australian history. In 1931 2FC (soon also part of the ABC) broadcast a talk about the Lambing Flat riots of 1861, in which white diggers had attacked Chinese goldminers (*Wireless Weekly*, 1931). In 1933–4 the ABC published a series of talks by Sheila Wigmore, later involved with the National Council of Women, on "Australian Pioneer Women". In her introduction, Lady Isaacs identified the four subjects—Lady Franklin ("wife of a governor in Hobart"), Mrs Baxter ("wife of a Chief Justice"), Lady Forbes ("wife of a squatter") and Mrs Campbell ("wife of a police magistrate")—via their husbands. They were, Wigmore contended, an "inspiration to the women of the present day" in Australia's "forward march", suggesting that Australian history should also be viewed as a narrative of national development and progress (Wigmore, 1933–4).

Sydney's Catholic station, 2SM, was particularly bold in its programming. In 1934 it seems to have broadcast some sort of re-enactment of Governor Arthur Phillip's explorations of 1788, together with a play about bushrangers by John Pickard. The New South Wales Department of Education visited 2SM's studios to observe the production of Brereton McKey's *Milestones of Australian History* and apparently advised students to listen to the plays (*Wireless Weekly*, 1934b, 1934c). By 1936 2SM was broadcasting *Tapestries of Life* at 9 pm on Mondays, featuring characters such as John Macarthur, "The Knight of the Golden Fleece" (*Wireless Weekly*, 1936c). In 1943 2CH presented every Tuesday and Wednesday night *Australian Cavalcade*, a drama produced by Edward Howell for Amalgamated Wireless Australasia (AWA) ranging from the settlement of the colony in 1788 to the landing at Gallipoli in 1915 (*Radio Pictorial of Australia*, 1943). Some more contemporary world history was also dramatised on the commercial airwaves. In 1942 *March of Time*, produced by R. C. Hickling for Melbourne's 3DB and relayed interstate, celebrated its 300th episode; the first had apparently been a prologue to the Spanish Civil War (*Radio Pictorial of Australia*, 1942).

In 1933–4 Captain Fred Rhodes, a master mariner, began supplying what he described as "historical anniversaries" to the fledgling ABC. His own regular columns for the Rockhampton *Morning Bulletin* on nature study, history and tales of the sea had led to him becoming associate editor of the newspaper and its weekly, the *Central Queensland Herald*. Some of Rhodes' broadcasts almost certainly focused on aspects of Australian history, which he viewed as "history without war"—later disputed by Frank Clune and academic historians such as Henry Reynolds (1982)—and characterised by a "wealth of adventure" (McDonald, 1988, pp. 368–9). Preoccupied with progress, like some of the other Australian broadcasters we have encountered, Rhodes deemed history important so that the county could learn from the past how best to build for the future. But while he was sympathetic to demands that the youth of Australia be taught Australian rather than "old-world" history, he deplored frequent inaccuracies in Australian history books during a lecture on "Our History Standards" delivered over 2BL in 1935 (*Central Queensland Herald,* 1935).

John Creighton at 2GB, and Captain Rhodes at the ABC, represent two types of historical broadcasters during the interwar years: professional radio announcers, and self-taught historians. There was a third category, occupied by academic historians. They belonged to the group, generally known as "news commentators", who were a distinctive feature of the Australian public and private airwaves from the late 1920s (Griffen-Foley, 2009, pp. 323–7, 363–7). Although *Wireless Weekly* remarked in 1936 that "playful professor[s]" were "pleased to be let off the academic chain", it criticised their talks for being boring and smug; this inspired a listener to write in defending as engaging the talks of G. V. Portus, a pioneer of adult education and professor of politics and history at the University of Adelaide (*Wireless Weekly,* 1936a, 1936b).

The academic historians who had the highest media profiles during these years were Ernest Scott and S. H. Roberts. Scott, professor of history at the University of Melbourne from 1913 until his death in 1939, was what today would be called a public historian or intellectual, with his voice carrying into schools, the press and public discourse. Originally a journalist, Scott became during World War I a conspicuously contemporary historian, endeavouring in his writings and his teachings to discern the contemporary in the historical. Even thought he tried to insist that daily newspapers could not be "dignified with the name of History", there is a sense in which the divide between his own historical work and his ongoing journalistic writings began to narrow (Macintyre, 1994, pp. 80, 172–4; Torney-Parlicki, 1999, p. 249). He was one of a group of individuals from respectable Melbourne who petitioned the new conservative United Australia Party government in 1931 to organise broadcasting upon an independent basis; the ABC came into being a year later (Inglis, 1983, p. 17).

Roberts, from 1929 second Challis professor of history at the University of Sydney (Australia's oldest), increasingly expanded his interest in international history to international affairs. He presented *Notes on the News* for the ABC from 1932 and, having published the runaway bestseller *The House that Hitler Built* in 1936, wrote frequently on foreign affairs for the *Sydney Morning Herald*, sounding loud and early warnings about Nazi Germany's ultimate intentions. During the war, as "Our Own International Correspondent", he wrote almost daily columns for the *Sydney Morning Herald* analysing the pattern of the Allied war effort, as well as weekly columns under his own name. It is notable that after his Hitler study he undertook no further scholarly writing, with his role as pundit taking over from that of professor (Schreuder, 1995, pp. 132, 143; 2002; Souter, 1981, p. 170). In an address to the New South Wales Country Press Association in 1950, Roberts advocated the establishment of a Diploma of Journalism. He also asked the press to co-operate in telling readers what the university was doing because, he insisted, "we have left the ivory tower" (*Sydney Morning Herald,* 1950).

Other historians were also heard on-air. The Oxford-educated Max Crawford, who returned to Sydney during the Great Depression to teach in high schools, found some stimulation making weekly broadcasts on the new ABC. He later succeeded Scott at the University of Melbourne (Anderson, 2005, pp. 31–2; Dare, 1995, p. 179). Brian Fitzpatrick was heard regularly on 3XY in Melbourne and the ABC in the 1940s and 1950s, although probably more in his capacity as a civil libertarian than as a historian (Serle, 1996).

Like other Australian "experts", historians were surely grateful for the opportunity to disseminate to a wider audience the insights and opinions gleaned from their research. Contributing to the media also served to augment their salaries, even though it is not entirely clear how profitable their radio broadcasts were. When Portus broadcast first on a commercial station in 1929, he was surprised to learn that no fee would be offered and tried, unsuccessfully, to persuade the manager that academics were professionals, just like musicians (Portus, 1953, pp. 243–4). Ernest Scott found churning out signed book reviews and unsigned editorials for the Melbourne *Argus* and the *Australasian* at three guineas a piece more lucrative than contributing to fledgling radio stations; when a station offered him £1 for each appearance on air, he tossed the letter into the wastepaper basket (Macintyre, 1994, pp. 145–6). Roberts, however, made considerable additional income from his public writings and broadcasts (Schreuder, 1995, p. 133).

Other individuals with training in history found places at the ABC. B. H. Molesworth, a lecturer in economic history at the University of Queensland, became Controller of Talks in 1937. Rohan Rivett, a young history graduate, wrote news bulletins for the ABC's shortwave service during the war (Inglis, 1983, pp. 57, 80, 191).

The electronic media also played a role in the memorialisation of Anzac Day. Just weeks after the landing at Anzac Cove, a re-enactment was staged at Tamarama beach in Sydney for Alfred Rolfe's film, *The Hero of the Dardanelles*. In 1928 the footage, which many people thought was real, was used in another film, *The Spirit of Gallipoli* (Byrnes, 2004). On 22 April 1937, Frank Clune dedicated his talk in *The Way of Adventure* series on the ABC's 2BL to "The Storming of Hill 971", where he himself had been injured at Anzac Cove.[5] During World War II, Anzac Day was invoked to boost morale. In April 1942 the ABC invited C. E. W. Bean himself to mark the anniversary by speaking on "That Anzac Day and This" (Inglis, 1983, p. 99); in April 1943 Dr H. V. Evatt, the Attorney-General and Minister for External Affairs, used a broadcast to declare that Anzac Day demonstrated that "we cannot rest" (*Sydney Morning Herald,* 1943). In 1946 Frank Grose, better known to 2GB listeners as "Uncle Frank", began covering the dawn service for the ABC and its shortwave service, as well as for a relay of commercial stations; he would continue to do this for the next 40 years.[6] When the Western Australian feminist and peace activist Irene Greenwood introduced a new program, *Woman to Woman*, to 6PM and 6AM in April 1948, one of her first broadcasts concerned Anzac Day services.[7]

From the Sesquicentenary to Indigenous History

In the midst of all this, there was a key anniversary in 1938: the sesquicentenary of the British settlement of Australia. A spate of historical features in the media was augmented by a special flight from London to Sydney and back sponsored by the Sydney *Daily Telegraph*, the Melbourne *Argus* and the Brisbane *Telegraph* (*Daily Telegraph,* 1938a). Aviation, promising a mastery over the continent and an end to its isolation, was a glamorous industry and seen by the media as the quintessence of modernity (Trace, 2001). Little historical material and few displays had been put on show in 1888, but 50 years later

Sydney boasted three historical exhibitions and a parade of 120 floats covering Australia's illustrious past. The mainstream media were closely involved in organising the sesquicentenary celebrations, and in ignoring the convict "stain" on the country's past (McLennan, 2006, p. 135; Thomas, 1988, p. 80).

The 32-page supplement on white Australia's first 150 years that the *Daily Telegraph* published (1938a, 1938b, 1938c) was just one of many special newspaper supplements. The *Sydney Morning Herald*, *Smith's Weekly* and the *Bulletin* stressed "Men Who Blazed the Trail", "From Autocracy to Federation" and "Out of the Past". The *Sydney Morning Herald* did at least contain articles on people who complicated the simple narrative of progress and prosperity—trade unionists, bushrangers and "blackfellows" (Saunders, 1998, p. 102; also Foley, 1997)—and on May Day the *Labour Daily* celebrated the people's struggle for progress (Thomas, 1988). On the ABC in early 1938, talks were heard by Brian Fitzpatrick ("History of Everyday Things in Australia"), Dr F. Kingsley Norris ("Some Medical Histories"), Dr W. G. K. Duncan, G. V. Portus, Frank Clune, and Australian "pioneers" ("I Remember").[8] In September came a series entitled *Outstanding People and Events in Australian History* (*Wireless Weekly*, 1938).

The sesquicentenary made the writings of nationalists such as Clune—a larrikin memoirist and travel writer with an increasing interest in Australian history—particularly attractive (Bonnin, 1980, p. 68). One "offensively Australian" member of the council of the Historical Society of Victoria wrote to the ABC expressing his pleasure at "hear[ing] history served up to the public in his [Clune's] inimitable style".[9]

In 1938 the writer, polemicist and former Rhodes scholar, P. R. ("Inky") Stephensen, who had just started a long and lucrative career as Clune's ghost-writer, wrote a short history of Australia for a special issue of his monthly magazine, *The Publicist*. It documented 150 years of Australia as a "Pommy" colony and "terrible atrocities against the blacks". Stephensen also helped to organise a "Day of Mourning" on Australia Day, 1938 (Horner and Langton, 1987, pp. 29–35; Munro, 1984, pp. 178–9, 183). A manifesto on citizen rights for Aborigines by the Aborigines Progressive Association and published by Stephensen contained a condemnation of the "popular Press" for making "a joke of us by presenting silly and out-of-date drawings and jokes of 'Jacky' or 'Binghi', which have educated city-dwellers and young Australians to look upon us as sub-human" (Aborigines Progressive Association, 1938). On 23 February there was a single ABC talk, by the pseudonymous "Offsider", acknowledging indigenous dispossession: "The Aborigines Lose a Continent".[10]

However, the attention drawn to Aboriginal disadvantage in 1938 may have backfired. When the editor of the Melbourne *Herald*'s magazine, John Hetherington, commissioned Frank Clune to write an article, accompanied by photographs, about his visit to Central Australia the following year, Hetherington insisted: "not pictures of [A]borigines please because we are rather tired of [A]borigines in this office".[11]

Clune was to emerge as the most popular historian in mid-twentieth century Australia. His combination of rich historical detail, talks with old timers on his extensive travels as a tax accountant, sense of place, and dialogue (some of it invented) found an eager market. Clune was not just an author, tourist and historian, but a multi-media personality. He and Stephensen worked hard to leverage the value of the scores of books published under Clune's name, using them as the basis for lengthy series of talks on the ABC (where his "dinkum Aussie voice" caused some consternation) and commercial radio, newspaper and magazine feature articles and serials (often syndicated). In 1948 the self-published *Frank Clune's Adventure Magazine* also appeared (Griffen-Foley, 2011). Clune's pacy historical narratives generally focused on romantic, heroic and mildly salacious subjects: explorers, bushrangers, "wild colonial boys", a notorious 1886 pack rape, and so on (Croft, 1993; Griffen-Foley, 2011).

For all the liberties he took with his sources, Clune took historical research seriously, and helped to open up both the subject of Australian history, and original sources for its study. In one of his earliest books, aptly entitled *Dig*, he wrote of assiduous archival "digging" and exploration (Clune, 1944, foreword). The story of the conquests of Australian pioneers in "opening up and taming" New Guinea, Clune told the ABC in 1943, deserved to be liberated from "dusty archives".[12] In a tribute to his friend, the poet Bartlett Adamson (1944) observed that Clune insisted on going to "fountain-sources for historic data, to original documents, original records"; his histories were "interfused with the personality of the historian" as he wove together "past and present with easy informality".

In his influential ABC Boyer Lectures in 1974, the anthropologist W. E. H. Stanner referred to a range of books about Australian history written between 1939 and 1955 to lament "the great Australian" silence about Aboriginal history. Clune's prolific works were not mentioned by the professor. Ann Curthoys (2008, pp. 233–50) has recently concluded that the representation of Aboriginal history in general works had become marginal in the period considered by Stanner. But in recognising that this had not always been so, and that there had also been some interest in Aboriginal history outside the academy, Curthoys herself has not engaged with Clune's historical writings.

As Margriet Bonnin (1980, p. 240) demonstrates, in the 1930s descriptive Australian writers, of whom Clune was one, popularised humanitarian and anthropological interest in Aborigines. He was comparatively early to recognise what he called, in the late 1940s, the "frontier wars". In a magazine story from around 1948 of the battle that had occurred between police, colonists and Aborigines in Roebuck Bay in Western Australia in 1864, Clune acknowledged that such accounts were rare in Australian historiography: "Perhaps we are nowadays becoming ashamed of some of the barbarities perpetrated by the pioneers" while taking Aborigines' "country away from them by force".[13]

Newspaper History Pages

In 1945 a Sydney afternoon newspaper, the *Daily Mirror*, introduced a historical feature as a more extended item than general news, usually related to the war. In a study (1991, pp. 198–207) and later compilation (1995) of the feature, Paula Hamilton found that each subject was woven into a racy dramatic story which had to have an "angle"; when a major political or sporting figure, or an eccentric, died, the editor tried to organise a historical feature on their life; and, perhaps most importantly, the feature had a much closer relationship to histories produced by the academy than she had at first suspected.

History pages were relatively common in Australia's metropolitan and provincial newspapers. From 1948 to 1951, for instance, the *Central Queensland Herald* published series of articles by Captain Rhodes under the pseudonym "Historicus" (McDonald, 1988). In the 1950s Dr Douglas Pike, who had been recruited to the University of Adelaide by G. V. Portus, needled the establishment by writing a series on "Early Adelaide with the lid off" for the morning *Advertiser* (Calvert, 2008, p. i; Nairn, 2002).

Even more unusual was *The News Way*, a monthly newspaper that made its debut in January 1948. It was published by Shere Khan Production Pty Ltd, based in Sydney and named after Rudyard Kipling's fictional tiger, and edited by a C. R. A. Riley, about whom little is known. The first issue, dated 26 January 1788, with "UNIQUE IN THE WORLD" and "Extra Ordinary Edition" above the masthead, reported on the arrival of the First Fleet in Sydney Harbour. The disclaimer that the newspaper was "NOT registered at the G.P.O. [General Post Office], Sydney, for transmission by post as anything", probably compounded the impression that *The News Way* was a spoof (*The News Way*, 1948a). However, it was actually a serious attempt to publish, and promote interest in, Australian history. Editions, all based on key dates over the preceding 160 years, contained "Stop Press" items about details of the settlement; a serialised cartoon based on Marcus Clarke's famous novel, *For the Term of His Natural Life*; historical quizzes with cash prizes; and advertisements from nineteenth-century Sydney newspapers.

Successive issues of "Australia's Only Historical Newspaper" became ever more insistent in calling for teachers and education departments to subscribe to the newspaper (*The News Way*, 1948b, 1948c, 1948d, 1948e). But although the education departments of New South Wales and Victoria, which had reacted uncertainly to the newspaper at first, had withdrawn objections to the newspaper by the 11th edition (*The News Way*, 1948g, 1949a), *The News Way* was struggling to attract enough subscriptions to keep afloat and to cope with the postwar shortage and cost of newsprint (*The News Way*, 1948b, 1948f). When Frank Clune, who bought and kept most editions, wrote a letter of congratulations ("should be in every home") for the next edition, the editor replied: "Thanks, Frank! What about a mite of publicity in some of your multifarious writings and sessions?" (*The News Way*, 1949a, p. 8).[14] *The News Way*'s 15th edition, in August 1949, was its last (*The News Way*, 1949b).

In spite of *The News Way*'s failure, there was something of a market for history writers for metropolitan newspapers, particularly in Sydney, by the 1950s. The journalist Leo Kelly specialised in history features for Sydney newspapers, including the *Sun*, in the 1950s and 1960s (e.g. Kelly, 1957). Soon after his arrival in Australia in 1949, the experienced British journalist and war correspondent, William Joy, also began contributing a historical feature page to a Sydney afternoon newspaper. In 1958 he moved to Consolidated Press, where he wrote history features for the Sydney *Sunday Telegraph* and, at times, its stablemate, the *Australian Women's Weekly* (Joy, 1961, 1962, 1964). Hamilton (1991, p. 205) notes that the volume of Australian material gradually increased in the *Daily Mirror*'s historical feature from the 1960s, and this was also the case at the *Sunday Telegraph*. Joy concentrated on Australian history, and Consolidated Press published Joy's *The Birth of a Nation: the story of early Australia*, specially commissioned by the *Sunday Telegraph* (1962). Imprints associated with the firm went on to publish series of historical books by Joy, as well as a portfolio of works by artists who sailed with Captain James Cook (Joy, 1964, 1972), suggesting that the mainstream media found Australian history of increasing commercial appeal.

In 1968 the *Daily Mirror* reproduced pages of the *London Gazette* documenting Cook's voyages; in the lead-up to Australia Day, 1969, the *Daily Mirror* published the names of 1000 convicts from the First Fleet, as well as supplements printed in the style and prose of the eighteenth and nineteenth centuries (*Daily Mirror*, 1969). The regular historical feature lives on in the *Daily Telegraph*, the newspaper with which the *Mirror* merged in 1990. The feature, which now includes an "On This Day" column (Hamilton, 1991), is edited by Troy Lennon, who has an MA in history from Macquarie University in Sydney. This sense of functionalism is present on radio, too, with the past neatly packaged in features such as the three-minute *It Happened This Day* spot produced by Fairfax Radio Syndication.[15]

History on the Australian Broadcasting Commission

As late as 1965, the secretary of the Queensland branch of the Women's Christian Temperance Union, Mrs M. C. Wadsworth, argued that broadcasting must have a moral purpose, advising the Australian Broadcasting Control Board that "the true function of television and radio is to help us raise a generation with strength of character and courageous leadership". Consequently, broadcasting stations should include sessions featuring "great examples from the Bible, and from history, biography and literature".[16]

ABC radio continued to produce one-off historical series, sometimes accompanied by booklets, as well as programs for schools. In 1963 the ABC published a periodical, *First Fleeters*, based on ABC talks. The ABC also worked with the National Trust to produce a 12-part series on heritage projects and problems in south-eastern Australia (ABC, 1969). Talks by the palaeontologist Edmund Gill (1967) on *Melbourne Before History Began* were followed *Melbourne on My Mind*, featuring oral history interviews with prominent male citizens including journalist and author Keith Dunstan, poet Chris Wallace-Crabbe and composer George Tibbits (ABC, 1976c). Half of secondary schools in New South Wales turned on *History for Form IV* in 1972 (Inglis, 1983, p. 317). There were also ABC series on *A History of Australian Painting* and *A History of Australian Architecture* (ABC, 1976a, 1976b). Australia's cultural history was further explored in *The Corrugated Violin Show*, a 10-part series, based on songs from different periods, targeted at children (Shortis and Nicholson, 1976). Brian Furlonger (1979) of ABC Public Affairs Radio presented a 15-part series on the history of Aborigines and the land, entitled *Kunapipi—The Earth Mother*, and introduced by an Aboriginal actor and playwright, Bob Maza.

In 1959 the ABC's board began nominating prominent Australians to present annual lectures on major cultural, scientific and social issues. Several of the Boyer Lectures, as they became known, were presented by historians: Professor W. G. K. Duncan (1962); Professor Sir Keith Hancock (1973); Professor C. M. H. Clark (1976); Bernard Smith (1980); Professor Geoffrey Bolton (1992); Dr Inga Clendinnen (1999), the only woman; and Professor Geoffrey Blainey (2001).[17]

In terms of internal ABC politics, it was the proposed Boyer Lectures of Manning Clark in 1976 that provoked the most dissension. He was no stranger to the media or to controversy, with his impressions of the Soviet Union following a visit there inspiring vigorous exchanges in the pages of the *Age*, the *Bulletin*, the *Observer* and *Tribune* in 1959–60, and the merits of his volumes of *A History of Australia* that appeared from 1962 being debated in the press (Holt, 1982, pp. 155–9; pp. 179–84). Following Clark's public criticisms of the Governor-General's sensational dismissal of the Labor government in 1975, a Liberal backbencher questioned the propriety of the ABC's invitation, and an ABC executive effectively proposed censoring Clark's Boyer Lectures. The idea was overturned due to a public outcry, and Clark went on to give five vividly personal talks about the making of a historian (Inglis, 1983, pp. 397–9; Jones, 1976; *Sydney Morning Herald,* 1976a, 1976b).

Historians as Public Intellectuals

In 1976 Manning Clark also became probably the first Australian historian to be the subject of a profile in the *Australian Women's Weekly* (Matthews, 2008, pp. 464, 507). His goatee beard, Akubra hat and sometimes prophetic public utterances were to make him a familiar media presence and the most high-profile historian in Australia. After his death in 1991, Clark was to become a central figure in Australia's history and culture wars, centred on the interpretation and teaching of the history of the British colonisation of Australia and the treatment of indigenous Australians. The *Courier-Mail* and the *Australian*, both part of the Rupert Murdoch/News Limited stable, were key protagonists in these public debates (Clark, 2008; Macintyre and Clark, 2003; Matthews, 2008, pp. 474–6). Another prominent, and often contentious, historian was Professor Geoffrey Blainey, who triggered a public debate about immigration in 1985, and himself became a recognisable media brand (Fraser, 2003).

There were other, more benign figures. Philip Geeves, an announcer with AWA and a returned serviceman, collaborated with a former teacher on a history of the Sydney suburb of Rockdale in 1954. This led to him presenting a historical feature, *Streets of Sydney*, on 2CH, where he was now program director, for 15 years, followed by *Moments in History* (Liston, 2007).[18] In response to a request from the Royal Australian Historical Society (RAHS), which he had joined in 1950, Geeves published *Local History in Australia* in 1967 on methods of research (Liston, 2007; Whitaker, 2001, pp. 72–3).

Geeves retired from commercial radio in the 1970s because of ill health, but continued to work on a history of AWA and in 1972 was honoured with a Fellowship from the RAHS for his extensive service to the organisation. He took on various historical commissions, including casual programs (as presenter, writer and/or producer) for ABC radio (Liston, 2007). From 1978 he presented a regular segment as "resident historian" on *City Extra*, Caroline Jones' morning program in Sydney. Both on- and off-air, he answered queries from the scores of letters he received each week, especially about family history.[19] The popularity of this spot encouraged the Macquarie Network to commission quiz shows on Australian history for 2GB in Sydney and 4BH in Brisbane, and led to Geeves himself being commissioned to write historical articles for *Woman's Day* and other publications.[20]

In 1980 Geeves also contributed to the sesquicentenary features of the *Sydney Morning Herald* and began writing a "Geeves on Thursday" column for the venerable newspaper.[21] As he observed in a lecture, "ancestor-hunting has become one of Australia's most popular hobbies" due to the appeal of *Roots* and the release of official Australian convict records, and in the lead-up to Australia's bicentennial in 1988.[22] After his death in 1983, a trust was established to fund a History Research Training Scholarship (*Sydney Morning Herald*, 1983). (Importantly, as the Aboriginal activist Gary Foley (1997) noted, the *Sydney Morning Herald* made significant concessions to indigenous people in its representations throughout the 1988 celebrations, showing how far it, and popular understandings of Australian history, had progressed since the newspaper's tokenistic efforts of 1938.)

Another popular historian to emerge through the commercial media was Peter Luck. In 1979 the journalist produced, co-wrote and presented *This Fabulous Century*, a 36-part television series on the Seven Network that used archival film and interviews with 300 Australians.[23] The Logie Award-winning series preferred the narrative over the analytical, had a strongly nostalgic appeal, and was a presenter-driven exploration of the past. Paul

Kelly, a respected journalist, editor and author, wrote and presented a five-part series, *100 Years: the Australian story*, on ABC television in 2001 (ABC, 2001).

Throughout this period the journalist and broadcaster Tim Bowden was working for the ABC's Department of Radio and Drama Features. In the early 1980s he was allowed to develop with the historian Dr Hank Nelson oral history-based documentaries such as *Taim Bilong Masta—The Australian Involvement with Papua New Guinea* (1981) and *Prisoners of War—Australians under Nippon* (1984). In 1985 Bowden founded the ABC's Social History Unit, which produced *Talking History*, a weekly magazine program; *Word of Mouth*, a 15-minute interview series; and *The Feature*, a half-hour documentary slot (Bowden, 2002, pp. 335–6; 2003, pp. 11, 22). The unit continues today, producing *Hindsight*, the only feature program on Australian radio devoted exclusively to social history, for Radio National. The unit's executive producers have included Dr Jane Connors, who has a doctorate in Australian history, and Michelle Rayner, who has an MA in public history from the University of Technology, Sydney.[24] Part of the significance of the Social History Unit's productions may lie in their recognition as new *sources* for Australia's academic and other historians.

Media audiences themselves could also generate sources. In 2003, for instance, the ABC television current affairs program *Lateline* invited viewers to help "uncover our nation's great untold stories". The History Challenge was introduced by Dr Michael Cathcart, on secondment to the ABC from the University of Melbourne,[25] and Emeritus Professor Frank Clarke, a regular on Radio National (Clarke, 2003). In 2006 Radio National also began producing *Rear Vision*,[26] looking at the historical context of current events in the news, for broadcast each Sunday afternoon (Inglis, 2006, p. 557).

Conclusion

When the words "history" and "media" are mentioned now, they probably bring to mind, for most Australians, the "living history" shows *The Colony* (SBS, 2005) and *Outback House* (ABC, 2005), or maybe ABC television's 2004 series, *Rewind* (Arrow, 2007). However, the *history of history* in the Australian media is a much longer one. Although the media was a notable omission from Macintyre and Thomas' *The Discovery of Australian History, 1890–1939* (1995), there has been some valuable Australian scholarship on the journalist as historian, the *Daily Mirror* historical feature, living history shows and historical drama (Cunningham, 1989; Moran and Keating, 2007; Turner, 2001), as well as on the relationship between film and history (Hughes-Warrington, 2007). Overall, however, as Williams (2008, p. 9) recently noted in an international survey, "research into the media's representation of the past has been limited".

This article has surveyed, for the first time, other aspects of history in the Australian press and on radio. Historical features in Australian newspapers were published to commemorate major anniversaries. These special features—some of which came to be augmented by radio specials—helped to create a national narrative around Anzac Day, and celebrated the British settlement (not "invasion") of Australia and the former penal colony's progress. They were augmented by regular features in metropolitan and regional newspapers, which focused increasingly on Australian history, and, by the 1960s, indicated that Australian history had some commercial appeal to the buyers of newspapers and associated book publications.

The press and radio allowed Frank Clune to popularise his histories in particular and Australian history more generally. The kind of history that he wrote, and that typically found its way into the Australian media, was nationalistic, nostalgic, romantic and heroic, and privileged the narrative over the analytical. Even so, from the 1930s and 1940s, a thread of awareness about indigenous dispossession and the frontier wars was also running through the work of Clune and some other contributors to the Australian media.

New history features in the press and on television further entrenched the role of the public historian/intellectual, and provided diverse opportunities for Australian academic historians, journalists and broadcasters to popularise and explore the past. They also, as Michelle Arrow (2006) notes in relation to presenter-driven television programs, reinforced the public image of an Australian historian as male and middle-aged (see also Hughes-Warrington, 2007, p. 127). It seems inevitable that there will be a preponderance of military history documentaries in the lead-up to the centenary of World War I and Gallipoli in 1915.

There are many other issues and questions that could fruitfully be pursued beyond the constraints of this Australian survey. If the media played an integral role in the propagation of the Anzac legend, what is the relationship between the media and other anniversaries such as Australia Day?[27] Has the public image of the Australian historian changed since the days of Manning Clark and, if so, how? Do the types of history presented in the Australian media differ when presented by journalists and non-journalists? Why has Australia not produced a historian and filmmaker with the profile of, say, Ken Burns, Professor Simon Schama or Professor Niall Ferguson? What role has the Australian media played in politicising history and historians, particularly since the history and culture wars of the 1990s? How do academics and students of history use history in the media as a source? Finally, how might, or should, the nexus between Australian media practitioners, public historians and academic historians develop?

NOTES

1. Australian foreign and war correspondents to write contemporaneous accounts include H. S. Gullett, Alan Moorhead, Ronald Monson and Chester Wilmot.
2. The release of the "Murdoch letter" by the Public Record Office caused a sensation as late as 1968.
3. National Archives of Australia (NAA)/Victoria: MP522/1, 2GB, Main File, letter from A. E. Bennett to Chief Manager, *Telegraph & Wireless*, 7 April 1926.
4. I am grateful to Margaret Van Heekeren for alerting me to "Brin-ga".
5. National Library of Australia (NLA): MS 4951, Frank Clune Papers, Box 28, Folder 168, "The Storming of Hill 971", 22 April 1937.
6. Mitchell Library, State Library of NSW (SLNSW): ML MSS 3261, Frank Grose Papers, Box 1, Minutes of meetings of 2GB Community Chest, 1945–1949, The Anzac Dawn Ceremony of Remembrance Program, 25 April 1946; Minutes of meeting of Radio Community Chest, 11 May 1962; Synopsis of activities contained in annual report for year ended 30 June 1965.
7. Murdoch University Library, Perth: Irene Greenwood Collection, Box 9, untitled program schedule for *Woman to Woman*, 26–29 April 1948.

8. NLA: MS 4951, Clune Papers, Box 28, Folder 168, ABC National Talks Programme, January to April 1938.
9. NLA: MS 4951, Clune Papers, Box 10, Folder 57, letter from J. K. Moir to Clune, 28 November 1938.
10. NLA: MS 4951, Clune Papers, Box 28, Folder 168, ABC National Talks Programme, January to April 1938.
11. NLA: MS 4951, Clune Papers, Box 28, Folder 168, letter from John Hetherington to Clune, 20 November 1939.
12. NLA: MS 4951, Clune Papers, Box 10, Folder 57, letters from Clune to Charles Moses, 6 February 1940; Clune to Thomas Matthew, 8 October 1943.
13. NLA: MS 4951, Clune Papers, Box 28, Folder 168, *Short Story Magazine*, n.d. (c.1948).
14. NLA: MS 4951, Clune Papers, Box 210, Folder 7.
15. See http://www.fxrs.com.au/Programming-And-Services/Features/It-Happened-Today.aspx.
16. NAA/Western Australia: K308, WP/1/19 PART 1, ABCB Agendum, 1 June 1965.
17. See http://www.abc.net.au/rn/boyerlectures.
18. SLNSW: ML MSS 4256, Philip Leslie Geeves Papers 1841–1983, Add-on 1912, Box 1, Folder: Notes for talks . . ., Royal Australian Historical Society Nomination for Fellowship, 26 September 1972.
19. SLNSW: ML MSS 4256, Geeves Papers, Add-on 1912, Box 1, Folder: "Personal Matters", letter from Geeves to "Brian", 24 August 1977. For correspondence with listeners, see ML MSS 4256, Geeves Papers, Boxes MLK 3620–6, 3628.
20. SLNSW: ML MSS 4256, Geeves Papers, Add-on 1912, Box 1, Folder: "Personal Matters', letters from Ron Hurst to Geeves, 15 August 1979; Pat Dasey to Geeves, 19 November 1980.
21. SLNSW: ML MSS 4256, Geeves Papers, Add-on 1912, Box 1, Folder: "Personal Matters', letter from I. Hicks to Geeves, 20 November 1980; ML MSS 4256, Geeves Papers, Box MLK 3128, Envelope: Correspondence 1980, letter from Frances Pollan to Betty-Jane May, 14 July 1980.
22. SLNSW: ML MSS 4256, Geeves Papers, Add-on 1912, Box 1, Folder: Research in Progress, "Your Family Tree Begins With You!", n.d.
23. See http://www.peterluck.com.au/biography.
24. See http://www.abc.net.au/rn/hindsight/about/.
25. See http://www.abc.net.au/lateline/history.htm.
26. See http://www.abc.net.au/rn/rearvision/about/.
27. For a British case study of the centrality of patriotic values to the operations of the daily press, see Conboy (2008).

REFERENCES

ABC (1969) *The Essential Past*, Sydney: ABC.
ABC (1976a) *A History of Australian Architecture: an ABC radiovision feature for schools*, Sydney: ABC.
ABC (1976b) *A History of Australian Painting: a radio vision feature, art for secondary schools*, Sydney: ABC.
ABC (1976c) *Melbourne on My Mind*, Sydney: ABC.
ABC (2001) *100 Years: the Australian story*, http://www.abc.net.au/100years/TV_contents.htm.

ABORIGINES PROGRESSIVE ASSOCIATION (1938) *Aborigines Claim Citizen Rights*, Sydney: Publicist.

ADAMSON, BARTLETT (1944) *Frank Clune: author and ethnological anachronism*, Melbourne: Hawthorn Press.

ANDERSON, FAY (2005) *An Historian's Life: Max Crawford and the politics of academic freedom*, Melbourne: Melbourne University Press.

ARROW, MICHELLE (2006) "'I Want to Be a TV Historian When I Grow Up!': on being a *Rewind* historian", *Public History Review* 12, http://epress.lib.uts.edu.au/ojs/index.php/phrj/article/viewArticle/199.

ARROW, MICHELLE (2007) "'That History Should Not Have Been How It Was': *The Colony, Outback House, and Australian history*", *Film and History* 37(1), pp. 54–66.

BONNIN, MAGRIET R. (1980) "A Study of Australian Descriptive and Travel Writing, 1929–1945", PhD thesis, Department of English, University of Queensland.

BOWDEN, TIM (2002) "Shaping History Through Personal Stories", Seventh Annual History Lecture, History Council of New South Wales, Sydney, 12 September.

BOWDEN, TIM (2003) *Spooling Through: an irreverent memoir*, Sydney: Allen & Unwin.

BYRNES, PAUL (2004) "Over the Top", *Sydney Morning Herald*, 12 June.

CALVERT, J. D. (2008) "Douglas Pike (1908–1974): South Australian and Australian historian", MA thesis, School of History and Politics, University of Adelaide.

CENTRAL QUEENSLAND HERALD (1935) "Our History Standards", 13 June, p. 58.

CLARK, ANNA (2008) *History's Children: history's wars in the classroom*, Sydney: UNSW Press.

CLARKE, FRANK G. (2003) *Australia in a Nutshell: a narrative history*, Sydney: Rosenberg Publishing.

CLUNE, FRANK (1944) *Dig: a drama of central Australia*, Sydney and London: Angus & Robertson.

CONBOY, MARTIN (2008) "A Tale of Two Battles: history in the popular press", in: Siân Nicholas, Tom O'Malley and Kevin Williams (Eds), *Reconstructing the Past: history in the mass media 1890–2005*, London and New York: Routledge, pp. 137–51.

CROFT, JULIAN (1993) "Clune, Francis Patrick (Frank) (1893–1971)", in: *Australian Dictionary of Biography*, Vol. 13, Melbourne: Melbourne University Press, pp. 447–8.

CRYLE, DENIS (1990) "Press Culture and Journalism to 1930", *Continuum: The Australian Journal of Media & Culture* 4(1), pp. 12–21.

CUNNINGHAM, STUART (1989) "Textual Innovation in the Australian Historical Mini-series", in: John Tulloch and Graeme Turner (Eds), *Australian Television: programs, pleasures and politics*, Sydney: Allen & Unwin, pp. 39–51.

CURTHOYS, ANN (2008) "Stanner and the Historians", in: Melinda Hinkson (Ed), *An Appreciation of Difference: WEH Stanner and Aboriginal Australia*, Canberra: Aboriginal Studies Press, pp. 233–50.

DAILY MIRROR (1969) "Free Lift-outs", 17–21 January.

DAILY TELEGRAPH (1938a) "Clouston's Swoop: plans Darwin in 52 hours, N.Z. 91", 4 February, p. 1.

DAILY TELEGRAPH (1938b) "Special Colour Souvenir", 9 February, p. 2

DAILY TELEGRAPH (1938c) "High Praise for *Telegraph*'s Celebrations Issue", 10 February, p. 2.

DARE, ROBERT (1995) "Max Crawford and the Study of History", in: Stuart Macintyre and Julian Thomas (Eds), *The Discovery of Australian History, 1890–1939*, Melbourne: Melbourne University Press, pp. 174–91.

DICKENSON, JACKIE (2010) "Journalists Writing Political History", *Australian Journal of Politics and History* 56(1), pp. 105–19.

ELLIS, MALCOLM H. (1949) *The Garden Path: the story of the saturation of the Australian labour movement by communism*, Sydney: The Land Newspaper.

FLETCHER, B. H. (2005) "Bladen, Frank Murcott (1858–1912)", in: *Australian Dictionary of Biography*, Supplementary Volume, Melbourne: Melbourne University Press, pp. 33–4.

FOLEY, GARY (1997) "The *Sydney Morning Herald* and Representations of the 1988 Bicentennial", May, Koori History website, http://www.kooriweb.org/foley/essays/essay_11.html.

FRASER, MORAG (2003) "The Media Game", in: Deborah Gare, Geoffrey Bolton, Stuart Macintyre and Tom Stannage (Eds), *The Fuss That Never Ended: the life and work of Geoffrey Blainey*, Melbourne: Melbourne University Press, pp. 148–56, 192–3.

FURLONGER, BRIAN (1979) *Kunapipi—The Earth Mother: a history of Aborigines and the land*, Sydney: ABC.

GILL, EDMUND D. (1967) *Melbourne Before History Began*, Sydney, ABC.

GRIFFEN-FOLEY, BRIDGET (2009) *Changing Stations: the story of Australian commercial radio*, Sydney: UNSW Press.

GRIFFEN-FOLEY, BRIDGET (2011) "Digging Up the Past: Frank Clune, Australian historian and multi-media personality", *History Australia* 8(1), pp. 127–52.

HAMILTON, PAULA (1991) " 'Stranger Than Fiction': the *Daily Mirror* 'Historical Feature' ", in: John Rickard and Peter Spearritt (Eds), *Packaging the Past: public histories*, Melbourne: Melbourne University Press, pp. 198–207.

HAMILTON, PAULA (1995) *Pages of History: the best of the Daily Telegraph Mirror historical feature 1945–1995*, Sydney: HarperCollins.

HAMILTON, PAULA and ASHTON, PAUL (2003) "At Home with the Past: initial findings from the survey", *Australian Cultural History* no. 23, pp. 5–30.

HOLT, STEPHEN (1982) *Manning Clark and Australian History, 1915–1963*, Brisbane: University of Queensland Press.

HORNER, JACK and LANGTON, MARCIA (1987) "The Day of Mourning", in: Bill Gammage and Peter Spearritt (Eds), *Australians: 1938*, Sydney: Fairfax, Syme & Weldon, pp. 29–35.

HUGHES-WARRINGTON, MARNIE (2007) *History Goes to the Movies: studying history on film*, Abingdon: Routledge.

INGLIS, KENNETH S. (1983) *This Is the ABC: the Australian Broadcasting Commission, 1932–1983*, Melbourne: Melbourne University Press.

INGLIS, KENNETH S. (2006) *Whose ABC? The Australian Broadcasting Corporation 1983–2006*, Melbourne: Black Inc.

JONES, MARGARET (1976) "The Reluctant Prophet", *Sydney Morning Herald*, 9 October, p. 11.

JOY, WILLIAM (1961) "Christmas in Australia", *Australian Women's Weekly*, 27 December, pp. 25, 32.

JOY, WILLIAM (1962) *The Birth of a Nation: the story of early Australia, specially commissioned by the Sunday Telegraph*, Sydney: Shakespeare Head Press.

JOY, WILLIAM (1964) *The Aviators*, Sydney: Shakespeare Head Press.

JOY, WILLIAM (1972) *The Exiles*, Sydney: Shakespeare Head Press.

KELLY, LEO (1957) "The Old Man and His Camels Are Part of History", *Sun*, 2 May, p. 33.

KELLY, PAUL (1994) *The End of Certainty: power, politics and business in Australia*, Sydney: Allen & Unwin.

KELLY, PAUL (2009) *The March of Patriots: the struggle for modern Australia*, Melbourne: Melbourne University Publishing.

KERR, RUTH S. (2000) "Lack, Clem Llewellyn (1900–1972)", in: *Australian Dictionary of Biography*, Vol. 15, Melbourne: Melbourne University Press, p. 45.

LACK, JOHN (2005) "Buley, Ernest Charles (1869–1933)", in: *Australian Dictionary of Biography*, Supplementary Volume, Melbourne: Melbourne University Press, pp. 52–3.

LAMONT, R., (1983) "Jose, Arthur Wilberforce (1863–1934)", in: *Australian Dictionary of Biography*, Vol. 9, Melbourne: Melbourne University Press, pp. 523–4.

LEMON, BARBARA (2008) "Betty Olive Osborn", in: *The Women's Pages: Australian women and journalism since 1850*, Australian Women's Archives Project, http://www.womenaustralia.info/biogs/AWE3121b.htm.

LISTON, CAROL (2007) "Geeves, Philip Leslie (1917–1983)", in: *Australian Dictionary of Biography*, Vol. 17, Melbourne: Melbourne University Press, p. 427.

MACINTYRE, STUART (1994) *History for a Nation: Ernest Scott and the making of Australian history*, Melbourne: Melbourne University Press.

MACINTYRE, STUART and CLARK, ANNA (2003) *The History Wars*, Melbourne: Melbourne University Press.

MACINTYRE, STUART and THOMAS, JULIAN (Eds) (1995) *The Discovery of Australian History, 1890–1939*, Melbourne: Melbourne University Press.

MATTHEWS, BRIAN (2008) *Manning Clark: a life*, Sydney: Allen & Unwin.

MCDONALD, LORNA (1988) "Rhodes, Fred (1877–1964)", in: *Australian Dictionary of Biography*, Vol. 11, Melbourne: Melbourne University Press, pp. 368–9.

MCLENNAN, NICOLE (2006) "Eric Dunlop and the Origins of Australia's Folk Museums", *reCollections: Journal of the National Museum of Australia* 1(2), pp. 130–51.

MITCHELL, BRICE and RUTLEDGE, MARTHA (1986) "Mackaness, George (1882–1968)", in: *Australian Dictionary of Biography*, Vol. 10, Melbourne: Melbourne University Press, pp. 288–9.

MORAN, ALBERT and KEATING, CHRIS (2007) *Historical Dictionary of Australian Radio and Television*, Lanham, MD: Scarecrow Press.

MORRISON, A. A. (1969) "Coote, William (1822–1898)", in: *Australian Dictionary of Biography*, Vol. 3, Melbourne: Melbourne University Press, pp. 456–7.

MUNRO, CRAIG (1984) *Wild Man of Letters: the story of P. R. Stephensen*, Melbourne: Melbourne University Press.

MURDOCH, KEITH (2010) *Gallipoli Letter: the letter that changed the course of the Gallipoli campaign*, Sydney: Allen & Unwin.

NAIRN, BEDE (2002) "Pike, Douglas Henry (1908–1974)", in: *Australian Dictionary of Biography*, Vol. 16, Melbourne: Melbourne University Press, pp. 1–2.

PORTER, ANNE (1993) "Birtwistle, Ivor Treharne (1892–1976)", in: *Australian Dictionary of Biography*, Vol. 13, Melbourne: Melbourne University Press, p. 185.

PORTUS, G. V. (1953) *Happy Highways*, Melbourne: Melbourne University Press.

RADIO PICTORIAL OF AUSTRALIA (1942) "March of Time", 1 February, p. 7.

RADIO PICTORIAL OF AUSTRALIA (1943) "Australian Cavalcade", 1 January, p. 19.

RADIO PICTORIAL OF AUSTRALIA (1945) "Women in History", 1 March, p. 6.

REID, ALAN (1971) *The Gorton Experiment*, Sydney: Shakespeare Head Press.

REID, ALAN (1976) *The Whitlam Venture*, Melbourne: Hill of Content.

REYNOLDS, HENRY (1982) *The Other Side of the Frontier: Aboriginal resistance to the European invasion of Australia*, Ringwood, Victoria: Penguin.

ROBERTSON, W. ("BRIN-GA") (1928) *Coo-ee Talks: a collection of lecturettes upon early experiences among the Aborigines of Australia delivered from a wireless broadcasting station*, Sydney: Angus & Robertson.

SAUNDERS, KAY (1998) " 'Specimens of Superb Manhood': the lifesaver as national icon", *Journal of Australian Studies* 22(56), pp. 96–105.

SCHREUDER, DERYCK (1995) "An Unconventional Founder: Stephen Roberts and the professional-isation of the historical discipline", in: Stuart Macintyre and Julian Thomas (Eds), *The*

Discovery of Australian History, 1890–1939, Melbourne: Melbourne University Press, pp. 125–45.

SCHREUDER, DERYCK (2002) "Roberts, Sir Stephen Henry (1901–1971)", in: *Australian Dictionary of Biography*, Vol. 16, Melbourne: Melbourne University Press, pp. 104–7.

SERLE, GEOFFREY (1996) "Fitzpatrick, Brian Charles (1905–1965)", in: *Australian Dictionary of Biography*, Vol. 14, Melbourne: Melbourne University Press, pp. 177–80.

SHORTIS, JOHN and NICHOLSON, DEREK (Comp.) (1976) *The Corrugated Violin Show*, Sydney: ABC.

SOUTER, GAVIN (1981) *Company of Heralds*, Melbourne: Melbourne University Press.

SUTHERLAND, ALEXANDER and SUTHERLAND, GEORGE (1877) *History of Australia from 1606 to 1876*, Melbourne: George Robertson.

SUTHERLAND, GEORGE (1880) *Tales of the Goldfields*, Melbourne: George Robertson.

SYDNEY MORNING HERALD (1943) "Spirit of Anzac", 27 April, p. 4.

SYDNEY MORNING HERALD (1950) "Journalism Diploma Considered", 18 October, p. 5.

SYDNEY MORNING HERALD (1968a) "Gallipoli Letter Changed Course of War", 18 November, p. 1.

SYDNEY MORNING HERALD (1968b) "The Murdoch Letter", 18 November 1968, p. 8.

SYDNEY MORNING HERALD (1968c) "The Murdoch Letter", 19 November 1968, p. 8.

SYDNEY MORNING HERALD (1968d) "The Murdoch Letter", 20 November 1968, p. 8.

SYDNEY MORNING HERALD (1968e) "The Gallipoli Letter", 21 November 1968, p. 2.

SYDNEY MORNING HERALD (1976a) "Professor Clark Is Deeply Saddened", 5 October, p. 2.

SYDNEY MORNING HERALD (1976b) "Whitlam Bitter Over Attack on 'Patriot'", 6 October, p. 8.

SYDNEY MORNING HERALD (1983) "Advertisement: Philip Geeves Memorial Trust", 26 November, p. 11.

THE NEWS WAY (1948a) January (dated "26 January 1788").

THE NEWS WAY (1948b) c. March (dated "20 June 1790").

THE NEWS WAY (1948c) c. May (dated "13 January 1799").

THE NEWS WAY (1948d) 26 July (dated "30 September 1813").

THE NEWS WAY (1948e) 27 September (dated "21 October 1824").

THE NEWS WAY (1948f) 25 October (dated "10 December 1828").

THE NEWS WAY (1948g) 30 November (dated "5 November 1830").

THE NEWS WAY (1949a) 14 February (dated "26 January 1836").

THE NEWS WAY (1949b) 29 August (dated "26 March 1846").

THOMAS, JULIAN (1988) "1938: past and present in an elaborate anniversary", *Australian Historical Studies* 23(91), pp. 77–89.

TORNEY-PARLICKI, PRUE (1999) "The Australian Journalist as Historian", in: Ann Curthoys and Julianne Schultz (Eds), *Journalism: print, politics and popular culture*, Brisbane: University of Queensland Press, pp. 245–58, 315–18.

TRACE, KEITH (2001) "Aviation", in: Graeme Davison, John Hirst and Stuart Macintyre (Eds), *The Oxford Companion to Australian History*, Melbourne: Oxford University Press, p. 54.

TURNER, GRAEME (2001) "Television, Historical", in: Graeme Davison, John Hirst and Stuart Macintyre (Eds), *The Oxford Companion to Australian History*, Melbourne: Oxford University Press, pp. 633–5.

WHITAKER, ANNE-MAREE (2001) "Fellows, 1901–2001: biographical notes on the fellows of the RAHS", *Journal of the Royal Australian Historical Society* 87(1), pp. 59–87.

WIGMORE, SHEILA (1933-4) *Australian Pioneer Women*, Sydney: ABC.

WILLIAMS, JOHN F. (1999) *ANZACS, the Media and the Great War*, Sydney: University of New South Wales Press.

WILLIAMS, KEVIN (2008) "Flattened Visions from Timeless Machines: history in the mass media", in: Siân Nicholas, Tom O'Malley and Kevin Williams (Eds), *Reconstructing the Past: history in the mass media 1890–2005*, London and New York: Routledge, pp. 7–28.

WIRELESS WEEKLY (1931) "Talks to Tune In", 13 February, p. 10.

WIRELESS WEEKLY (1934a) "Saves You Trouble", 18 May, p. 8.

WIRELESS WEEKLY (1934b) "One More Mile", 3 August, p. 7.

WIRELESS WEEKLY (1934c) "Touring the World", 21 September, p. 12.

WIRELESS WEEKLY (1936a) "Editorial: The Professors", 7 February, p. 14.

WIRELESS WEEKLY (1936b) "The Professors", 21 February, p. 15.

WIRELESS WEEKLY (1936c) "Tapestries of Life", 14 August, p. 43.

WIRELESS WEEKLY (1938) "All This Talking", 22 July, p. 7.

YOUNGER, RONALD M. (2003) *Keith Murdoch: founder of a media empire*, Sydney: HarperCollins.

ZWAR, DESMOND (1980) *In Search of Keith Murdoch*, Melbourne and Sydney: Macmillan of Australia.

THE PRESENCE OF THE PAST
The uses of history in the discourses of contemporary South African journalism

Herman Wasserman

Since the demise of apartheid in South Africa, the media landscape has undergone significant shifts that impacted on journalism practice. Among the most important of these shifts was the setting up of a system of self-regulation to ensure ethical journalism in the new free democratic environment. The normative frameworks upon which this system rested have, however, been highly contested, and subjected to much debate. In mounting a defence against what has been seen as ongoing attacks and threats to press freedom, journalists often invoked history to validate their normative positions and to assert their professional values and identities. This article draws on semi-structured interviews with South African journalists to explore their attitudes towards the impact of South African journalism history on current practices and professional ideologies. The aim is to establish the ways in which apartheid history is used to make meaning in post-apartheid professional debates.

Introduction

The demise of apartheid in South Africa brought important shifts in the composition of the country's media industry as well as to the professional practices of journalists. South African journalists found themselves having to reorient their professional practices and occupational ideologies—the sum of ideas and views on social and political issues through which journalists validate and give meaning to their work (Deuze, 2005, p. 446)—in an environment that was undergoing rapid socio-political changes. Coupled with the tectonic shifts in the local socio-political landscape were radical changes in the news industry globally. These global shifts occurred partly as a result of advances in new media technologies that redefined journalism practices, and partly as a result of global flows and contraflows in media capital and content that allowed new relationships between the local and the global to emerge (cf. Thussu, 2007).

During this reorientation, South African journalists frequently found themselves at odds with political stakeholders over the appropriate normative framework within which their journalistic practice should be couched. In the ensuing debates and conflicts—continuing after a decade and a half of democracy—journalists often drew upon recollections of South African journalism history to shape and/or validate and justify their normative positions. These appeals to the past may be contrary to the more common association of journalism with the present rather than the past. Journalism is most often seen as concerned more with the "here-and-now than with the there-and-then", with the past seen as falling outside journalists' self-definition of their work (Zelizer, 2008, p. 80). Journalists' "treatment of the present often includes a treatment of the past" (Zelizer,

2008, p. 81), and therefore journalists' role as "memory agents" need to be taken more seriously. Journalists contribute to the construction of social memory through the subjects they report on, weaving together not only significant news events but also the smaller narratives of everyday life (Kitch, 2008, p. 313).

This article wants to illustrate, via a South African example, how journalism's memory work extends beyond the construction of the past through news narratives in reportage to the definition of professional ideologies and identities in the way journalists invoke the past to reflect on their own role and position in society. Conboy (2010, p. 6) re-iterates the point that the "sedimentations of its past practice" continue to influence journalism even as it reorients itself towards the future. The relationship of journalists with the past is malleable and dynamic, and the memory work they engage in often takes the form of collective reconstruction of the past to serve their own agendas (Zelizer, 2008, p. 81). In the South African journalism discourses that will be examined in this article, the agenda being served by a collective reconstruction of the past relates largely to threats experienced in the present. South African journalists draw on the past to defend themselves against what is perceived as pressures on their professional freedoms. This practice is in line with Deuze's (2005, p. 446) observation that the appeal to ideological journalistic values becomes especially pertinent when journalists are faced with public criticism. The appropriation of historical narratives by South African journalists—both in interview scenarios where they reflect on their professional identities and in the practice of reporting on media freedom issues—can therefore be seen as facilitative of a process of reconstructing journalism practice in the post-apartheid era. By positioning themselves in relation to a collectively reconstructed past, journalists gain discursive traction in deploying the ideological values of independence, freedom and surveillance of power to ensure journalism's special status in post-apartheid South Africa (cf. Deuze, 2005, p. 447).

This article seeks to explore how appeals to history are used by South African journalists in reconstructing professional norms and identities after apartheid. It explores the discursive positions taken up by journalists as these relate to current debates about journalism's role in a new African democracy. It poses two central questions: (1) What normative influence do South African journalists see the past exert on their current practice, especially in terms of their relationship with the political sphere? and (2) How do constructions of South African journalism history feature in journalistic self-identification discourses?

The article seeks to answer these questions through a thematic exploration of a set of in-depth, semi-structured interviews conducted with journalists to gauge their attitudes towards the past and their views of the role journalism should play in the post-apartheid democratic political sphere. Before embarking on this exploration, a brief background to the post-apartheid South African journalism landscape will be given. This background is needed in order to contextualise the self-identification of South African journalists in relation to the country's past and the changes occurring in the journalism landscape since democratisation.

Background

In the negotiations and contestations surrounding journalism's role in the post-apartheid socio-political context, two aspects regularly top the agenda: the composition of the industry (in terms of both the racial composition of newsrooms as well as the political economy of ownership, access, and control) and the efficacy of the press self-regulatory system. In both these areas, significant shifts have taken place since democratisation, yet questions remain as to whether these shifts have been far-reaching enough to effect transformation of the media, and whether these shifts were made in the right directions. These questions have given rise to an ongoing normative debate about South African journalism practices and values, and sometimes result in clashes between journalists and the government and/or the ruling party (the African National Congress and its alliance partners).

The first changes to the composition of the South African news media industry occurred during the 1990s as a result of both external and internal developments. Externally, the South African media's re-entry into a competitive global economy after years of isolation required local outlets to embark on cost-cutting and increased profit-seeking. The end of trade and economic sanctions following the demise of apartheid in the 1990s led to a process of interpenetration of local and global media capital (Tomaselli, 2000, p. 279). South African conglomerates such as Naspers became global players while foreign-owned companies like Independent plc took ownership of local outlets. White and black media capital merged as a result of a series of "black empowerment" and "unbundling" deals (Tomaselli, 2000). The re-entry of South Africa into the global market therefore brought about a complex set of global–local flows and contraflows that altered the political economy of journalism in the country, and futher afield on the African continent as South African companies extended their reach (Teer-Tomaselli et al., 2007, p. 153).

Despite what can be called the deracialization of the structures of media capital, the underlying commercial logic of the press remained the same, and news media markets continued to be largely racially segmented. The "oligopolistic tendencies" in the print news media and the legacy of apartheid in the racialized ownership of media houses complicated the debates about what journalism's role should be in transforming South African society (Horwitz, 2001, p. 283). Questions arose as to whether structural inequality in the press has been sufficiently addressed and whether this restructuring would significantly broaden access to the public sphere (Tomaselli, 2000, p. 288). During the transition period in the 1990s, strong calls for a press that would assist in the transformation of the country came from the liberation movements, even if there was no clear African National Congress (ANC) policy on the press "beyond broad assurances of press freedom" (Horwitz, 2001, p. 284). The tension between differing views of what journalism's role should be in transformation of South African society, and how such transformation relates to ownership of news media, is one that continues to characterize normative debates about South African journalism.

Internally, the shift from the apartheid regime's authoritarian control of the news media to an environment where the news media enjoyed Constitutionally guaranteed freedoms, was coupled with the development of a self-regulatory mechanism for journalism. To ensure ethical standards and pre-empt the intervention feared from the new majority government, a Press Ombudsman (later expanded into a Press Council) was established, alongside a statutory body for complaints in the broadcasting sector, the Broadcasting Complaints Commission (BCCSA). The normative framework underpinning this self-regulatory process was based in the liberal consensus among news media institutions, grounded in individual rights, a free-market commercial environment and ethical codes largely taken over from the North, in which journalism's "watchdog" function was emphasized. Tensions between this normative conception and contrasting views which saw journalism's role in more nationalistic and developmental terms became evident early in the transitional period (see Wasserman, 2006, for a more detailed discussion).

Furthermore, the clear ideological lines that characterized the press landscape during apartheid became blurred. The result of the above-mentioned complex range of shifts in media capital and professional demographics meant that journalism was to an extent freed of the ideological moorings of apartheid. The high degree of political parallelism between the apartheid state and its sympathizers in the Afrikaans press, the liberal parliamentary opposition and its advocates in the mainstream English press, and anti-apartheid activists and the alternative press, made way for the politics of the free market, where old political allegiances became redundant and commercially unviable (Tomaselli, 2000, p. 287). But new lines of opposition opened up—mostly between the press and the government, dominated by the ANC. Even as newsrooms adapted to become more representative of the country's demographic, opposition between the press and the government seemed to mount anew. Because of the dominance of one party on the political landscape, journalists often saw themselves performing a *de facto* political opposition, even while in daily practice there seemed to be an emerging symbiosis between journalists and political elites (Wasserman, 2010). This oppositional stance taken by journalists, defined in terms of appeals to liberal-democratic normative frameworks and concepts such as the "Watchdog" role, can be seen as a major contributing factor to the tensions between the media and the ruling party (see Wasserman and De Beer, 2005, for a discussion of some of these conflicts). While conflicts about the normative role of journalism in post-apartheid society largely focused on journalism practice—the perceived unprofessional conduct of journalists in terms of their ethical codes—the political economy of the news industry was never far away from these discussions. Issues around ownership, access and journalism's publics continue to take a central place in debates about journalism's role and function in this new democracy.

A recurrent criticism against South African journalism during the first decade of democracy has been that it represents sectional instead of national interests through its privileging of white viewpoints and experiences. Even before he assumed the first democratic presidency, Nelson Mandela pointed to the white, middle-class make-up of press ownership and editorial staff (Mandela, 1994). One of the earliest clashes between the news media and the post-apartheid government centred around debates about newsrooms' lack of representation of the racial composition of the country. A (methodologically flawed) investigation conducted in 1999 by the South African Human Rights Commission into racism was met with "scorn and incredulity" by journalists, who responded with discursive strategies of denial of racism (Durrheim et al., 2005) and saw the investigation as an incursion on their newly found press freedom. State interventions included the Employment Equity Act that requires businesses (including the news media) employing more than 50 people to transform their staffing complement according to race and gender demographics of the country. Through the Skills Development Act the state aimed to broaden skills and learning activities, *inter alia* through the establishment of Sector Education and Training Authorities (SETAs). All these interventions raised important questions for journalism training, education and employment in the context of transformation (Steenveld, 2002, p. 9).

The liberal-democratic consensus upon which the post-apartheid press based its professional ideology has been challenged on a number of occasions as being inappropriate for a developmental, transitional democracy. These challenges to the self-regulatory system came to a head in 2010 when the ruling ANC resurrected an earlier proposal for a statutory Media Tribunal that would have a stronger monitorial role and greater powers of sanction over journalists than the current self-regulatory Press Council has. In addition, a Protection of Information Bill was proposed, which would allow government officials to classify documents as containing sensitive information and therefore inaccessible to journalists and the public. While these moves were in all probability motivated by unwelcome criticism and exposés of corruption in the news media, the criticism of journalists was couched rhetorically in terms of development, access and participation in the specific context of a transitional African democracy. The current self-regulatory system was seen as inadequate and biased towards the journalistic establishment rather than the broader public. The latest criticism, in 2010, of the news industry as being "too white and too commercial" came from the ANC, in a proposal to establish a Tribunal with tougher powers to sanction journalists and an appeal to Parliament to look into ownership and control of the print media (Boyle, 2010).

While these debates relate directly to the current role and position of journalism in post-apartheid society, today's pressing questions cannot be divorced from history. In current normative debates, history has often been used as a weapon in the arsenal of the respective protagonists. In defending their freedom, journalists have frequently pointed to the recent history of Constitutional negotiations, historic utterances by struggle icons such as Nelson Mandela[1] or a reconstructed past in which the media's role to bring down the apartheid regime was foregrounded. Critics of the news media in turn pointed to the less glorious aspects of South African journalism history, such as the skewed racial profile of the journalistic workforce, the complicity of some sections of the news media with the apartheid regime and the limited, liberal critique offered by others.

The question arises as to how these historical references were embedded in a broader discourse about normative roles for journalism in South Africa. How did the reconstructions of journalism history serve current agendas? What impact do these reconstructions have on current journalistic practices? This article seeks to identify themes in journalistic constructions of the South African past as they emerge in contemporary normative debates, and to relate these constructions to underlying journalistic self-identifications and positioning towards the post-apartheid political sphere. The aim of this exploration is to understand how recollections and reconstructions of the past shape journalists' professional identities and function strategically in their everyday practice.

Approach and Method

This article explores how South African journalists reconstruct history as part of a process of defining professional values, identities and ideologies in the post-apartheid context. The article is interested in how memory work performed by journalists serves a contemporary agenda, namely to defend journalism against threats to journalistic freedom, and to redefine the role of journalism within the contested normative sphere in post-apartheid South Africa. While the memories of past practices and professional values are reconstructed in the present—therefore flexible and subject to interpretation (cf. Zelizer, 2008, p. 81)—these reconstructions are rooted in new ethical and legal frameworks of professional bodies of journalists (such as the South African National Editors Forum) and the state. While the reconstructions therefore enter a contested normative space, they are not merely imaginings without any material context.

Journalists' perception of how the past impacts on their contemporary journalistic values and practices was explored by means of a range of interviews conducted with political journalists working in various media across the country. These interviews formed part of a larger, comparative transnational study on political communication in new democracies, funded by the British Academy (LRG-45511), which covered: Southern Africa (Namibia, South Africa), East Asia (Taiwan, South Korea), Eastern Europe (Bulgaria, Poland) and Latin America (Brazil, Chile). Between eight and ten political journalists, working for a range of media including commercial and public media, across print, broadcast and online, were interviewed in each of these countries, in addition to interviews with politicians and intermediaries (whose responses are not included here). The study was aimed at exploring the interaction, relationships, expectations, values and norms of these three sets of actors, and their views of the media's role in post-apartheid democracy. Questions were organized into five major categories: orientation towards the democratic system; perception of own role and of counterpart; news production; relationship between media and government/politicians; and personal characteristics. After data collection, the responses were coded and analysed using a codebook that again was developed collaboratively between the researchers representing various regions, in order to obtain an analytical tool that could be applicable in a cross-country comparison. This article draws on questions that probed interviewees' understanding of the influence of South African history on the current work, also (where applicable to the interviewee) as regards to their assessment of working as a journalist in post-apartheid South Africa as compared to under apartheid. Although these interviews took place in 2008 and 2009, before the latest confrontation between journalists and the ruling party around a proposed Media Tribunal, respondents were asked to reflect in overarching terms about the relationship between the media and government, about their interpretations of notions of media freedom and responsibility (see Wasserman, 2010) and about the extent of transformation that has taken place in the news media since democratization. This article draws in particular on the interview question "Do you think that the recent past still has an influence on the way in which the media report on politics in South Africa?", but also situates this question within the responses received from journalists to other, more general questions. Journalists' responses to this question can provide insight into the way in which reconstructions of history operate within an interpretive community and form part of collective "struggles for determining meanings among groups of social actors" (Berkowitz and TerKeurst, 2006, p.125).

The responses from journalists on questions of how the past continues to influence their work can give us insight into how history is interpreted as well as re-inserted into contemporary visions of professional practice, and help us understand the norms governing the relationship between journalists, politicians and the public in a new democracy. Space does not permit to engage here in a content analysis to indicate how these attitudes towards the past are reflected in journalistic texts. However, it may be assumed that journalists draw on the idealized recollections of the past as found in the interview scenarios (as will be discussed in the following section) in their practice. Examples of how the past is used in journalistic practice to support contemporary agendas may be found in recent reporting around the statutory Media Tribunal proposed by the ruling party as an alternative to the existing self-regulatory system. A particularly productive discursive strand in current normative debates is one in which journalism is seen as having offered resistance to apartheid and contributed to the fall of the regime. This construction of a heroic past, with journalists seen as "martyrs" (Trewhella, 2010) for the struggle still forms part of journalistic identities in the present. This construction of history (which usually omits the support given to the apartheid regime by Afrikaans sections of the press, nor mentions the limits to the liberal critique offered by the English-language press under apartheid) is mustered to resist the renewed pressures from the democratic government on the press, which some (e.g. Fourie, 2002, 2009) have compared to the repression of freedom of speech by the Nationalist government. When editors of liberal newspapers in the apartheid era are therefore characterized as having "spent decades opposing press censorship", it is with the purpose of validating their attack on the current proposals by the ANC-led government for a Media Tribunal and a draft Protection of Information Bill as evidence of "ignorance of the lessons of the past" (*Mail and Guardian*, 2010a).

In defending the current self-regulatory system, the Press Ombudsman (who leads this professional body) is presented as a "veteran journalist with almost 50 years' experience" (*Mail and Guardian,* 2010c), i.e. someone associated with an idealized journalistic past and who himself has defied previous onslaughts to press freedom. In reporting on a statement by international news agencies decrying the Media Tribunal proposal, their invocation of an idealized journalistic past is also highlighted (*Mail and Guardian,* 2010d): "The media in South Africa and foreign reporters working in the country told the world about the horrors of apartheid, despite intimidation, attempts at censorship and attacks by the white-led government". Critics that likened the proposed Tribunal and another piece of legislation, a proposed Protection of Information Bill, with the draconian control of the press under apartheid, received prominence in news reports (e.g. *Times Live*, 2010a, 2010b). These examples suggest that the reconstructions of the past as found in journalists self-defining discourses (to be discussed below), may also influence journalistic practice in the way that reports on media freedom issues are framed.

Interview Responses

In the responses offered by journalists to the question on how the recent past continues to shape their contemporary practice, three broad themes were identified. In each of these themes, history was linked to journalism in a particular way that has implications for current normative views and professional attitudes. Several respondents remarked on the fact that history continues to influence the way they select and approach news stories. What exactly that history is, how it continues to influence their work, and how history should shape normative views of journalism in the current dispensation, were articulated differently by various journalists. Depending on which view of South Africa's media history dominates, various roles for journalism in post-apartheid society were envisaged.

History as a Battlefield: Journalism as Resistance

Although the Tribunal and the Protection of Information Bill were not yet mooted at the time of the interviews for this study, the following remarks from a journalist who had worked under apartheid and continues to do so as a senior journalist in the post-apartheid era, exemplify the professional identity of journalists as providing resistance to repression and therefore justified to claim special status (cf. Deuze, 2005, p. 447) in the post-apartheid context:

> I think that you [could] have libel laws that govern public mores and a sense of right and wrong but no, I can't see a case [where you could justify restrictions on media freedom] . . . Having lived through Apartheid where we had attempts to muzzle us, but at the end of the day the Apartheid regime was not big enough to resource and maintain the kind of oppressive system and regime that it believed it could. [T]here was a very interesting period in the late 1980s where they brought in emergency regulations and it used to take us ten days to two weeks to drive a coach and horses through them, and then we had them bring more. I think that is another thing worth emphasizing: the history of a very vibrant and vigorous press in this country even during the depths of Apartheid. Visitors always expressed some amazement at the degree of criticism that came out despite a plethora of laws and regulations and all sorts of stumbling blocks that were put in our way. We nevertheless were able to keep going hammer and tongs at the government.

This journalist did go further to lament the fact that young journalists in the post-apartheid era are less able to articulate such a clear professional vision, as they have exchanged a strong political identity for one in service of commercial goals—thus acknowledging pressure on journalistic independence from within as well as from without the industry.

Other pressures coming from within the journalistic community itself were seen as linked to cultural sensitivities. Journalists often remarked on subtle pressures by politicians and officials in the post-apartheid era. While these pressures were not always overt, and sometimes based in certain cultural expectations, some journalists remarked on the ways in which cultural frames of reference may shape journalists' response to these threats. Cultural notions of respect may inhibit journalists or lead to self-censorship:

> [I]n the past, even if you would dare, you were very aware of the danger of the state coming down on you or imprisonment or public case being closed down and stuff like that. Now . . . the Constitution guarantees you freedom of speech, for instance, but you do get some government officials or ministers who always try to find a way to silence you. Even if they know they are going to lose in court, they will still try . . . it comes down to intimidation really. . .

> I think what you'll find is it's really more to do with culture or tradition . . . in the African society. You don't question your elder and you don't show disrespect. So often you'll find that journalists are talking amongst each other, [saying] "we should really ask him this or that" but they wouldn't, because they allow their culture to influence them and to dictate to them on, as to how or if they should ask a specific question. . .

History as a Wound: Journalism as a Cure

The South African past was frequently seen by journalist respondents in this study as something to escape from, or to be healed from. Journalism itself, as it was practised under apartheid, was sometimes seen as part of the problem, since it was cast in terms of the mistakes committed by journalists at the time—not speaking out clearly enough against apartheid, allowing themselves to become drawn in too close to power, not asking tough enough questions. In contrast, journalism in the post-apartheid era is projected in terms of the opportunity it provides to rectify some of these mistakes and provide a cure for the wounds of history. Journalism can also play an educational role by reminding the public of this hurtful and unjust past, and finding ways of ensuring that history does not repeat itself. The lessons that journalists view as important to learn apply to normative aspects of journalism practice—such as making sure that journalism does not again succumb to political power—but also to journalism's relationship to society as a whole. Consider this response from a journalist when asked what the media's responsibility should be towards the citizenry:

> It's a broader question around democracy and the extent to which we open up public debate around crucial issues in South Africa, but do it in a way which is not necessarily divisive and is not necessarily negative, or constantly negative in its approach ... In South Africa what we [are] trying to do, one of the goals, is of course nation-building by trying to heal divisions of the past. The issue is: are our media and our politics aiding that, or is it actually furthering that divide? You know in some critical areas I think that ... it's difficult for the media, because they've got to sell newspapers, and they've got to sensationalize certain things, and at the same time there are a lot of challenges and problems in South Africa and a lot of crises as such that need to be reported on. The issue is how do we strike that balance?

Another respondent pointed to the history of racism in South Africa to justify certain limits to the Constitutional guarantees to press freedom in the post-apartheid era:

> [T]here must be free flow of information in the public interest for the democratic process to flow. And obviously, there are confines to this: privacy, decency, the fact that you cannot extend your freedom to harm that of another, and no incitement especially given our history of racial hatred, and then no incitement to violence, that sort-of basic things.

In this conceptualization, history continues to impact on normative debates in the present as a curtailment on journalistic excesses. A knowledge of journalism history could therefore encourage journalists to take greater responsibility in how they use their freedom, and could also provide a source of learning for journalists and publics alike. Journalism can facilitate this learning process firstly by reminding publics of the country's history—especially the youth who have grown up in a free society and may not be fully aware of the historical context in which the democratic society came into being. But journalists themselves can also form a community of practice to constantly remind themselves of historical mistakes so as to avoid committing those mistakes again. Said another journalist:

> [W]e have a certain history. Our history is not the same as many other countries. So when we write we have to sort of keep that at the back of our minds. We don't have to continuously remind ... people. People know. But now and then, based on our history,

depending on what the issue is, we have to remind in our reporting, also state the fact that we don't need to have that type of situation again, we need to also educate our readers that the people, especially the young people of today, so that many of them are fully sympathetic to what happened ... we need to educate them ... [to know] that what they have is because of our history ... our struggle ... people who have struggled to where we are today.

Once such historical knowledge is achieved, it would impact on how journalists report on politics in the post-apartheid context. Knowledge of apartheid history will enable journalists to take a more critical stance and not take information received from government at face value:

> If you don't understand the history of the country then your reporting is going to be a little bit skewed ... you will just play it straight ahead and you will become a conduit. This is what government says and you will report on it. You have to have a grip on ... the history of this country. Some people don't accept it, unfortunately, but it's a fact that ... a political journalist would not be able to do a proper job unless [you have a solid knowledge of history].

As another journalist put it:

> I think the media was, I think our papers were the tools in the hands of the previous regime. I think the past experiences would make us more wary of [repeating] that [situation] so to an extent it [works] to our advantage.

From the above responses it can be seen how the normative roles envisaged for journalism in the current, post-apartheid society are validated through an appeal to history, albeit a history that should not be repeated. The litmus test for a socially responsible journalism in the post-apartheid era, in this vision, is the extent to which it succeeds in healing the "divisions of the past", cementing over the fractures of the citizenry and enabling journalists and citizens alike to draw on historical lessons in order to avoid repeating them. Notable in this regard is also how this social responsibility role is seen as something to be fulfilled in spite of the political economic pressures in a commercialised post-apartheid media landscape. Healing the divisions of the past is a goal to be strived for in spite of the pressures of having to "sell newspapers" and having to "sensationalize certain things".

History as Presence: Journalism as Continuity

A substantial part of the criticism by the post-apartheid government is based on the notion that the post-apartheid press is still too elitist, and that self-regulatory mechanisms are not accessible to the poor majority (see, for instance, president Jacob Zuma's suggestion that a proposed Media Tribunal will act "on behalf of" the poor; *Mail and Guardian*, 2010b).

However, some journalists acknowledged the continuity between journalistic practices and attitudes from the apartheid to the post-apartheid era, even as they differentiated between different generations of journalists. For these respondents, journalism's history is not purely heroic, and journalism is not easily rid of that history.

On this view, journalistic attitudes have not necessarily changed equally rapidly as the structure of the media industry did. For these respondents, democratization is still an incomplete process as far as journalistic mindsets are concerned. In terms of demographics, the inequalities of the past have also been seen to continue to dog post-apartheid newsrooms, despite progress that has been made in terms of racial and gender representation:

> Our newsrooms are a lot more representative of the demographics than they used to be. But the people who control copy, the transformation is a lot slower there. You have a lot of women journalists who are doing a lot of hard work but not a lot of us [women] are in decision-making positions. There has been a juniorization of newsrooms which has led to a lapse in quality. There has been a massive exodus of trained journalists which has resulted in a weakening of institutional memory. We often make very sloppy mistakes in the media and government accusations that often we are unable to explain complex processes around governance does have some merit. I think we don't take enough responsibility as media for that. On the other hand, we have also seen a rapid advancement of young people, of Black people and of women.

Another journalist pointed out that not all their colleagues "have gotten used to the freedom" of the news media in the new dispensation and continued to approach political news in a similar way as the 1980s, when sections of the press were either supportive or in collusion with the apartheid regime. The example used by this respondent was *The Citizen* newspaper which, during the 1980s, had been secretly funded by the apartheid government. Other respondents pointed to the public broadcaster, the South African Broadcasting Corporation (SABC), who in their view has been repeating the mistakes of the past by allowing interference by the current, democratic government in ways similar to that of the old regime.

Although these observations by journalists clearly served as a means to distance themselves from the way journalism had been practised in the apartheid era, they acknowledged that some continuity with the past remains, carried forward by journalists from one era to the next. While such generational continuity was viewed in a negative light, the introduction of a new cohort of journalists to newsrooms in an attempt to overhaul the industry was, on the other hand, also seen by this respondent as "certainly influencing capacity and age and experience of reporters" detrimentally. These comments were re-iterated by several other respondents, who remarked on new, junior journalists' lack of the historical and contextual knowledge required to report on complex political issues or to locate news events within broader historical trends.

These responses introduce a double position of journalists towards the past. While their understanding of press freedom and responsibility (see Wasserman, 2010) require of them a rejection of certain complicit journalism practices of the apartheid past, their professional identity (which places a premium on technical skills and values such as truth, accuracy and surveillance of power) leads them to be critical of the inadequacies of junior reporters which are seen as resulting partly from the hasty reconstitution of newsrooms in the post-apartheid era.

South African journalism history is therefore used in a contradictory way here—on the one hand, the ignominious parts of that history are rejected in an attempt to validate current practices and ideologies, while a golden era of journalistic skills is called into remembrance.

The continuities between the past and the present, as they play out in journalistic attitudes, routines and practices, problematize any glib notion of journalism in the democratic era as having made a clean break with the past. One senior journalist gave a sober assessment of the continuities between past and present attitudes and practices, but also saw these continuities as indications of a normative contestation that is dynamic because it is ongoing. Her response is worth quoting at length:

> Fourteen years in the life of a country is nothing. The contradictions in South Africa are becoming more stark. There was a democratic breakthrough in 1994 but the race and class faultlines are intensifying in many ways and the past is still festering in the present. That is apparent in a whole range of areas: in state institutions, in practices, etc. It is one thing to legislate a set of laws but you can't legislate attitudes—to change attitudes takes time and work. So I think the past is very present in the way political coverage is happening.
>
> [L]ook at the media's portrayal of every new ANC leader. When Mandela took over he was a saint, which to me was problematic, but when Mbeki had to take over there was this big exceptionalism around Mandela. There was no other person like him so how could Thabo Mbeki possibly fit his shoes? There was a lot of suspicion around Mbeki; he was an enigma, a silent assassin, etc. until he showed himself as an economic conservative and the checking classes were very happy with him—even though he proved to be quite undemocratic—but he became the person that we could not do without. We had outsourced our responsibilities to him as a leader. That was the basis of the argument that a fallible leader like Jacob Zuma couldn't possibly fill the shoes of the philosopher-king that is Thabo Mbeki.
>
> All of that is in fact prejudices parading as analysis and says more about the cultural preoccupations of the people raising the problem than it does about the subject.
>
> Just because we had a democratic breakthrough does not mean that these institutions are in good shape or that all your contradictions have been resolved—it's an ongoing process. That has become part of the fight over whether the settlement we had in 1994 was an appropriate settlement. That contestation is now in full swing. You have class fault lines, the division between the urban and the rural . . . It's quite a dynamic process in many ways.

Conclusion

From the responses by journalists it became clear that history continues to impact on current journalism practices and normative positions. However, there was no clear consensus on exactly how history should inform current normative positions. Three positions emerged from the way history was drawn upon to support normative positions:

- The past was celebrated—then journalism's perceived role in resisting apartheid became a justification for a renewed insistence on press freedom in order for journalism to act as watchdog over the post-apartheid government.
- The past was rejected—then journalism's social responsibility in the post-apartheid era was emphasized in order to avoid stepping into the same traps as before.

- No clear break between the past and the present was identified, but continuities between past and present practices were acknowledged. Instead of embracing post-apartheid journalism as inherently democratic, the persistence of inequalities and undemocratic attitudes were pointed out, while the loss of some professional values from the past were lamented.

While there was a general acceptance on a normative level that journalism in post-apartheid South Africa has to avoid repeating the mistakes of the past by asserting their freedom, independence and social responsibility, these values are not automatically reflected in practice. While, perhaps for strategic reasons, some journalists chose to emphasize the role that journalism played in resisting apartheid and therefore deserves special status and recognition in the post-apartheid dispensation (articulated through values such as "freedom" and "independence"), others were more critical. For the latter group, critical scrutiny of the relationship between journalism and democracy should be directed as much towards journalism as towards politicians and institutions of government.

The range of ways in which journalists understand history as having a bearing on current journalism practice and normative orientations, suggests that history should be studied with an open mind and a critical attitude in order for contemporary values, norms and practices to be informed by it. Using history as a mere validation of contemporary practices or a source for sloganeering, would be a simplistic and dishonest approach. Instead, normative debates in the present can only be enriched by historical perspectives if history is drawn upon in all its complexity and contradictions.

NOTE

1. In his acceptance speech of the African Editors' Forum's award (covered widely in the press, see e.g. IOLNews, 2010; Ndebele, 2010; *The Witness*, 2010) Njabulo Ndebele quotes from Mandela's 1994 speech mentioned earlier in this article (Mandela, 1994), but omits references to Mandela's stinging critique of the white-controlled ownership structure of the press at the time. This selective use of history is perhaps an indication of how sensitive any criticism of the press has become in post-apartheid South Africa, and how starkly the lines of debate are drawn.

REFERENCES

BERKOWITZ, DAN and TERKEURST, JAMES V. (2006) "Community as Interpretive Community: rethinking the journalist–source relationship", *Journal of Communication* 49(3), pp. 125–36.

BOYLE, BRENDAN (2010) "ANC's Media Tribunal Plan", *The Times*, 29 July, http://www.timeslive.co.za/local/article577048.ece/ANCs-media-tribunal-plan, accessed 11 November 2010.

CONBOY, MARTIN (2010) "The Paradoxes of Journalism History", *Australian Journalism Review* 32(1), pp. 5–13.

DEUZE, MARK (2005) "What Is Journalism? Professional identity and ideology of journalists reconsidered", *Journalism: Theory, Practice, Criticism* 6(4), pp. 442–64.

DURRHEIM, KEVIN, QUAYLE, MICHAEL, WHITEHEAD, KEVIN and KRIEL, ANITA (2005) "Denying Racism: discursive strategies used by the South African media", *Critical Arts* 19(1/2), pp. 167–86.

FOURIE, PIETER (2002) "Rethinking the Role of the Media in South Africa", *Communicare* 21(1), pp. 17–40.

FOURIE, PIETER (2009) "'n Terugkeer na die onderdrukking van vryheid van spraak? Ooreenkomste tussen die apartheidsregering(s) en die ANC se optrede teen die media" ["A Return to the Repression of Freedom of Speech? Similarities between the apartheid government(s) and the ANC's actions against the media"], *Tydskrif vir Geesteswetenskappe* 49(1), pp. 62–84.

HORWITZ, ROBERT B. (2001) *Communicaton and Democratic Reform in South Africa*, Cambridge: Cambridge University Press.

IOLNEWS (2010) "Mandela Honoured by African Editors' Forum", 15 October, http://www.iol.co. za/news/mandela-honoured-by-african-editor-s-forum-1.686613, accessed 11 November 2010.

KITCH, CAROLYN (2008) "Placing Journalism Inside Memory—and memory studies", *Memory Studies* 1(3), pp. 311–20.

MAIL AND GUARDIAN (2010a) "Media May Be Under Dire Threat Once More", 26 July, http://www.mg.co.za/article/2010-07-26-media-may-be-under-dire-threat-once-more, accessed 8 November 2010.

MAIL AND GUARDIAN (2010b) "Zuma: media tribunal to 'complement' self-regulation", 9 September, http://www.mg.co.za/article/2010-09-09-zuma-media-tribunal-to-complement-selfregulation, accessed 8 November 2010.

MAIL AND GUARDIAN (2010c) "Media Tribunal Would Be a 'Very Dangerous Move'", 30 July, http://www.mg.co.za/article/2010-07-30-media-tribunal-would-be-a-very-dangerous-move, accessed 14 January 2011.

MAIL AND GUARDIAN (2010d) "News Agencies Sound Warning Over Media Tribunal", 8 September, http://www.mg.co.za/article/2010-09-08-news-agencies-sound-warning-over-media-tribunal, accessed 14 January 2011.

MANDELA, NELSON (1994) "Address to the International Press Institute", Cape Town, 14 February, http://www.sahistory.org.za/pages/people/special%20projects/mandela/speeches/1990s/1994/1994_international_press_institute.htm, accessed 2 November 2010.

NDEBELE, NJABULO (2010) "Press Ever Onwards", *The Times*, 17 October, http://www.timeslive.co. za/opinion/article712471.ece/Press-ever-onwards, accessed 11 November.

STEENVELD, LYNETTE (Ed.) (2002) *Training for Media Transformation and Democracy*, Rosebank: The South African National Editors' Forum and the Independent Newspapers Chair of Media Transformation, Rhodes University.

TEER-TOMASELLI, RUTH, HERMAN WASSERMAN and ARNOLD S. DE BEER (2007) "South Africa as a Regional Media Power", in: Daya Thussu (Ed.), *Media on the Move: global flow and contra-flow*, London: Routledge, pp. 153–64.

THE WITNESS (2010) "Madiba Gets Editors' Forum Award", 16 October, http://www.witness.co.za/ index.php?showcontent&global[_id]=49164, accessed 11 November 2010.

THUSSU, DAYA (Ed.) (2007) *Media on the Move: global flow and contra-flow*, London: Routledge.

TIMES LIVE (2010a) "Ramphele: bill a haunting reminder of apartheid", 11 August, http://www.timeslive.co.za/Politics/article596688.ece/Ramphele--Bill-a-haunting-reminder-of-apartheid, accessed 14 January 2011.

TIMES LIVE (2010b) "ANC Wants to Mask Corruption: Zille", 18 September, http://www.timeslive. co.za/local/article665243.ece/ANC-wants-to-mask-corruption--Zille, accessed 14 January 2011.

TOMASELLI, KEYAN G. (2000) "South African Media, 1994–7: globalizing via political Economy", in: James Curran and Myung-Jin Park (Eds), *De-Westernizing Media Studies*, London: Routledge, pp. 279–92.

TREWHELLA, PAUL (2010) "No More Martyrs to Media Freedom in SA", *The Times*, 11 October, http://www.timeslive.co.za/iLIVE/article701709.ece/No-more-martyrs-to-media-freedom-in-SA, accessed 8 November 2010.

WASSERMAN, HERMAN (2006) "Globalised Values and Postcolonial Responses: South African perspectives on normative media ethics", *The International Communication Gazette* 68(1), pp. 71–91.

WASSERMAN, HERMAN (2010) "Freedom's Just Another Word? Perspectives on the media freedom and responsibility in South Africa and Namibia", *International Communication Gazette* 72(7), pp. 567–88.

WASSERMAN, HERMAN and DE BEER, ARNOLD S. (2005) "A Fragile Affair: an overview of the relationship between the media and state in post-apartheid South Africa", *Journal of Mass Media Ethics* 20(2/3), pp. 192–208.

ZELIZER, BARBIE (2008) "Why Memory's Work on Journalism Does Not Reflect Journalism's Work on Memory", *Memory Studies* 1(1), pp. 79–87.

FRAMING REVOLUTION AND RE-FRAMING COUNTER-REVOLUTION

History, context and journalism in the new left-wing Latin American paradigm

Jairo Lugo-Ocando, Olga Guedes, and **Andrés Cañizález**

The end of the 1990s marked the rise of left-wing governments in Latin America. Hugo Chávez in Venezuela, Luiz Inácio Lula da Silva in Brazil, Néstor Kirchner in Argentina, Evo Morales in Bolivia, among others, swept into power, in most cases in landslide victories at the polls, only to encounter almost immediately afterwards a forceful opposition from the mainstream and privately owned commercial news media. Evidence of this can be seen in the active role played by these news media outlets in the rapid overthrow of President Hugo Chavez in April 2002 and in the quasi-antagonistic relations between the media and the government in places such as Argentina, Bolivia, Brazil and Nicaragua. We argue that at the centre of this struggle is an appropriation of history by journalists and news editors which serves to contextualise and frame political news stories so as to provide specific meanings to current accounts and narratives. This, we argue, is in itself a crucial aspect of political power relationships during a period when the armed forces and traditional political parties no longer have the leverage they once had. This article assesses the extent to which journalists and news editors have been using history to frame the accounts and narratives in their news stories as a way of providing legitimacy to their political allies while undermining that of their foes. In so doing, it looks at specific cases in the region, while analysing news content during key events in recent years.

Introduction

The end of the 1990s witnessed the rise of left-wing governments in Latin America. Hugo Chávez in Venezuela, Luiz Inácio Lula da Silva in Brazil, Néstor Kirchner in Argentina, Evo Morales in Bolivia, were prominent among those who swept into power, in most cases in landslides victories at the polls, only to encounter almost immediately a forceful opposition, not least from the mainstream and privately owned commercial news media. Evidence of this can be seen in the active role played by these news media outlets in the rapid overthrow of President Hugo Chavez in April 2002 (Lugo and Romero, 2003) and the subsequent antagonistic relations between the news media and the government in places such as Argentina, Brazil, Bolivia and Nicaragua. We argue that at the centre of this struggle is the appropriation of history by journalists and news editors to contextualise and frame political news stories in ways which provide specific meaning to current accounts and narratives, demonstrating that editors can effect change by means of language (Schlesinger, 1978, p. 272). This is of paramount importance since the narratives of continuity and discontinuity within the news media can tend to obscure reality when historical context is used to frame politics in a selective manner, making it difficult for citizens to make informed decisions in order to express their political preferences and articulate their own political identities.

Indeed, this appropriation of meaning by the different political actors is a key aspect of access to power at a period when the armed forces no longer have the ability to intervene in specific situations and overthrow governments. Indeed, the power of the military has dramatically declined in Latin America in the past three decades, although arguably they continue to influence democratic governments across the region (Pion-Berlin, 2001, p. 3). Equally important to mention is the decline of traditional political parties, which have dramatically lost ground among an electorate which has become far more pragmatic in its voting preference over the years (Kitschelt et al., 2010, p. 309). This decline in power of the traditional institutions has been a consequence of multiple factors such as the end of the Cold War, the strengthening of newly democratic institutions, the increasing influence of the rule of law in the context of human rights and the inability of post-dictatorship regimes to fulfil the expectations of the electorate in terms of social and economic reform.

In light of this new scenario, power elites which now face government agendas that are directed at wealth re-distribution and that challenge traditional oligopolies by opening participation to the poor, are making use of privately owned commercial news media to confront these new left-wing governments. The elites, which in most cases either own these media outlets or have a very close relationship with their owners (Ferreira, 2006, p. 158), rely on these media outlets to help them articulate and mobilise opposition against the left-wing leaders now in power. The left-wing governments have responded to this by modifying legislation regarding news media ownership and regulating their activities. In some cases these governments have gone so far as to nationalise existing news media outlets at the same time as creating new ones in order to challenge prevalent accounts of events and counter-mobilise public opinion.

Consequently, this has translated into a new landscape in which each side has ended with news media provision that acts as quasi-political parties (Lugo and Romero, 2003). In the middle of this confrontation, journalists are obliged to become partisan players, while most spaces of balance and cohabitation have almost disappeared. Indeed, partisan journalism has become a prominent feature of the journalism of many countries in the region (Hughes, in Lugo, 2008, p. 145), even when some of these media outlets have attempted to strike some balance in such divided and antagonistic environments. In this polarised arena, journalists and editors from both sides have made use of their power to structure and articulate meta-narratives that can confer or undermine the legitimacy of their supporters or adversaries. Moreover, since legitimacy is a process, which is best described as a "second-order" objectivation of meaning that integrates the meanings already attached to disparate institutional processes (Berger and Luckmann, 1975 [1966], p. 110).

This article assesses the extent to which journalists and news editors have been using history to frame the accounts and narratives in their news stories as a way of providing legitimacy to their political allies, hence giving a new level of integrated meaning to the news stories, while undermining that of their foes. In so doing, it looks at specific cases in the region, while analysing news content during key media events in the past 10 years. The article acknowledges that there are many degrees of partisan journalism, all of which have their own respective narratives of "truth". It also realises that these practices take many different forms across the region. As a result of this, each one of them also makes selective use of historical memory and provides a different interpretation of historical context surrounding the explanatory framework of the news content. Indeed, it is argued here, the sole fact that journalists in Latin America are commonly deploying historical context in their narratives is a new phenomenon in the modern era. Hitherto, insufficient context and oversimplified interpretation of the events have been for a very long time the main criticisms of journalism in the region (Ford, 1999; Mujica, 2010 [1967], p. 240). There is a vast amount of research in Latin America from the 1970s and 1980s that suggest that providing historical concept was not a main feature of journalism and that this omission was systematic (Alvarez, 2010 [1978]; Díaz Rangel, 1991; Faundes, 1998). Therefore the key question to answer is why is this happening now? Why are journalists starting "to make" space and "air time" for historical context? Why is it so important to contextualise the events within historical narratives at this particular moment? How is this done and by whom? Is this contextualisation carried out in the same way by different journalists and news media outlets? Are there common trends to be identified in the region regarding these practices?

To assess the increasing use of historical context in framing news in Latin America, we have made use of a set of qualitative research techniques. This includes content analysis, Critical Discourse Analysis (CDA) and a close reading of a selected sample of coverage of key media events in Argentina, Brazil and Venezuela. In so doing, we aim to provide understanding of how this kind of framing is achieved by journalists working in the mainstream media and, more importantly, why and in which circumstances this is carried out. The media events in question are: the election of Dilma Rousseff in Brazil in 2010; the confrontation between President Cristina Kirchner and Papel Prensa in Argentina in 2010, and the coup against President Hugo Chávez in 2002. By formulating this initial analysis, we are calling for other researchers in Latin America to look at this area more closely in their own countries.

Theory on Yesterday and Today

Let us start by making a broad generalisation; history and journalism are two very similar activities in the sense that both selectively pick up certain facts only to then edit and frame them into a chosen context so they can, at the end, present a specific interpretation of reality. Therefore, the idea of an entirely objective history is as ludicrous as the notion of value-free objectivity in journalism. As suggested by Gaye Tuchman, objectivity is a "strategic ritual" (1972, p. 661), which acts as a chimerical illusion that invokes truth to gain legitimacy but that obviates a set of values and inherent biases in the construction of social reality. Indeed, on a daily basis journalists and historians behave as praetorian guards of imaginary frameworks of knowledge that confer power to groups and individuals by means of justificatory narratives. When referring to how political discourse is framed in the media, Lakoff highlights the term "metaphors" (2004, p. 3; 2008, p. 125) to indicate how political discourses are dominated by a variety of words and terms that say one thing but mean another. These metaphors create meaning within specific media contexts "in a time in which the media not only transforms reality, but also creates it" (Martin Barbero, 1996, p. 28).

However, it is important to remind ourselves that these metaphors have developed from historical narratives that are widely accepted among the public. In the United States, for example, the idea of the founding fathers and the conquest of the Wild West are widely used in legitimising quasi-imperial military action abroad as if this was a logical necessity of exporting "freedom" and other values associated with liberal democracy; in a quest against the barbarism of other, less progressive societies. Indeed, the dichotomy between "us", the civilized West, and the "barbaric" others, the enemy at the gate, is a prevalent notion in the discursive metaphors used by those in power or aspiring to it (Fitzgerald, 2007). Hence, any narrative that challenges the values of modernity, expressed in the notions of secular globalisation and liberal development, is categorised as an unsustainable utopia. Islamic radicalism, indigenous revolts and eco-anarchism are all seen and portrayed by the mainstream media as nothing more than deviant activities which, dangerously, do not fit in mainstream society and which in the most irrational manner demonstrate a "hatred of our way of life". After all, news stories do reflect reality, but one that is socially constructed (Soley, 1992, p. 12).

These ideological constructions have permeated and defined many of the prevalent journalistic discourses and news narratives in Latin America. As a result, news is framed by journalists and news editors in terms of the specific notions of modernity that are embraced by the West, where the values used by journalists as a framework for their stories are more often than not those of Western historical preference. In the debt crisis of the 1980s, for example, headlines and news stories referred to the millions of "US dollars" given by the Latin American nations as "wasted Marshall Plans" (Ramos, 1991, p. A15), even though most of the audience had no understanding of what that meant. In fact, news stories rarely had any explanatory historical context. Instead key media events were, for many years, reported and presented to the public based on "pure facts", deploying the claim of objectivity in order to ward off criticism (Tuchman, 1972, p. 662). During this time, these facts were narrated without reference to causes and roots, therefore offering a limited explanation as to why and how things had happened.

The reason is obvious; those who dominated politics and the mainstream news media outlets in Latin America at that point were, widely speaking, of the same colour, class and position in society. They shared histories and class interests. Therefore, media outlets and their narratives, with few exceptions, were an expression of prevalent power structures in the region (Loreti, 2005, p. 14). Hence, the construction of "news" needed to be an exercise of power in the crudest terms. References to national or regional history were almost non-existent and when they appeared they were spun to fit specific conceptions which would reinforce and legitimise existing power structures.

However, the status quo has suffered major transformations in recent years. The emergence of a new political class, made up of mostly left-wing civilians, former guerrilla fighters and former military commanders-turned-politicians has opened an important space for new voices and actors across the continent. The "villains of the past" are now in power and with them they have brought their own distinctive narratives. Discourses and facts needed to justify why those who were called "guerrilla fighters", "coup leaders", "anarchists" and "criminals" were now allowed to hold power. How could this be explained in the media? More importantly, how could this be explained in news media outlets, which until then had little to do with historical context and which had effectively made large swathes of society invisible? The answer would lie in providing historical context that in some cases would legitimise (and romanticise) the past actions of these left-wing leaders, while others reinforced their status as "villains" in a post-Cold War era.

The Case of Hugo Chávez

Indeed, one of Hugo Chávez's first gestures as president of Venezuela in March 1999 was to write and immediately leak to the press a letter of solidarity to Carlos Ilich Ramírez, alias "The Jackal", who was serving a life sentence in France for his terrorist activities in the 1970s. This "humanitarian gesture" provoked a debate that obliged the news media in Venezuela to backtrack in history and explain to a new generation who this man incarcerated in France actually was. For weeks, the media opposing Chávez started to include data from their own archives in their news stories and dispatches to tell people about the links of their newly elected president with this convicted terrorist and criminal. However, in doing so, the news media opened a Pandora's Box of histories and narratives that until then had remained tightly shut and which now allowed pro-government media voices to start building alternative frameworks for the news. Whether this was a gaffe or a well-considered strategy is irrelevant. What is clear, nevertheless, is that this event developed a snowball effect that helped to shift and re-frame the debate from the civic–military dichotomy to a left–right debate. Indeed, previous to that, news about Chávez would normally have referred to a "former military coup leader" now elected president. With this letter to Carlos Ilich Ramírez, president Hugo Chávez had effectively donned a more appropriate left-wing garment on top of his military robes.

The historical context used to frame news stories has used both modern and distant metaphorical memories. For the Chavismo, the initial rhetoric linked the current move-ment with the heroic actions of Simón Bolívar and the peasant revolt led by Ezequiel Zamora. Estrella Gutierrez, the then correspondent of Inter-Press Service in Caracas, puts this into perspective when writing about the elections: "The Venezuelans are witnessing a campaign of the 20th century dominated by discourses and symbols of the 19th century" (Inter-Press Service, November 12, 1998). For the opposition, the framing has tried to relate Chávez's leadership with the era of dictatorships in Latin America, while trying to revive anti-communism fears from the Cold War era among the wider public but with little apparent success.

The two main political media events for the legitimising narrative of Hugo Chávez happened in 2002; a coup that was shortly followed by a general strike. At this time, the government was able to overcome a fierce battle for the "public support wage" through the airwaves and front pages of the media in which pro-government and anti-government journalists were spinning history to their advantage. The content analysis of the news of this year and the remembrance of these events in the following years tell us a lot about the use of history by journalists. For example, in a sample of 62 articles published in April and May 2002 by the two main newspapers, which editorially supported the opposition to Hugo Chávez, *El Universal* and *El Nacional*, there was a consistent framing of the President as a former coup leader. The sample only included articles that were mentioned on the front page and that refer to news items related to the attempted coup (Table 1).

The analysis of the sample indicates a deployment of history to frame Hugo Chávez's presidency as not legitimate as it derived from a previously attempted coup. Indeed, 39 of the articles mention the fact that Hugo Chávez himself had led a failed coup against

Table 1
Number of articles that refer to news items related to the attempted coup, published in April and May 2002

Media outlet	Coup framing	Military framing	Using word "paratrooper"
El Nacional	18	29	7
El Universal	21	33	12

President Carlos Andres Perez in 1992 (from which base he built his popularity for years after) and all the articles mention, or at least suggest, that he himself was a military man, in some cases repeatedly using the word "paratrooper". Hernan Lugo, who covers politics for *El Nacional*, argues that this was a legitimate practice, as the public "had to be reminded that those denouncing the coup in 2002 were themselves protagonists of a previous coup in 1992".[1]

The practice of reminding the public of the sins of "the other" to highlight the lack of moral high ground to denounce present events is widely used by journalists all over the world. During the Gulf War of 2003, Al-Jazeera often used old footage of Donald Rumsfeld shaking hands with Saddam Hussein in the 1980s, even when this footage had no relevance in itself to the news item being broadcast other than highlighting their close relation in the past. This practice occurs in reverse to that of news interpretation and deconstruction, by providing an explanatory framework to the news item while constructing the story. The intention, of course, is to guarantee that the audiences ascribe a certain meaning and a certain interpretation to the news they read. Because of this, the pro-government camp has focused on de-constructing the framing of news related to the events of April 2002. In so doing, they have tried to create a different narrative in which audiences can "read between the lines". One of the most important of these efforts was the 2003 documentary, *The Revolution Will Not Be Televised*, directed by Irish film-makers Kim Bartley and Donnacha Ó Briain. By using a wider frame from a camera on top of a building the producers were able to counter the opposition's version of the events according to which Chávez's supporters were shooting against unarmed members of the public. This documentary made headlines inside Venezuela and abroad, setting a different record about the events to that provided by the coup leaders—who used their version to justify the coup. For several years after the coup, this documentary became one of the main referents to supporters inside Venezuela and abroad to highlight the role of the traditional Venezuelan media in orchestrating the coup.

For pro-government broadcast programmes and Internet news sites, such as *La Hojilla* and *Aporrea.org*, de-constructing the framing of news carried out by the pro-opposition media has become the news in itself. For these media outlets, what is important is not the news but the way it is reported. The programme *La Hojilla*, which is broadcast by the main government channel VTV, has been particularly influential in de-constructing news from the other camp by incorporating alternative historical facts when re-framing news. Many references made in the programme when de-constructing stories refer to excesses and abuses committed against left-wing leaders who were killed or disappeared in the 1960s and 1970s.

All these references shown in Table 2, without exception, were made in the context of current events happening in Venezuela. Special attention must be given to how these types of pro-government news media outlets tend to use the military coup against Salvador

Table 2
References to past political events in pro-government broadcast programmes and websites between April and May 2010

	References to 1960s and 1970s government excesses against political dissidents in Venezuela or in Latin America	Reference (including comparisons) to the government of and military coup against Salvador Allende in 1973	Other references to the 1960s and 1970s (including African independence movements, Vietnam War, etc.)
La Hojilla (on VTV)	31	12	62
Aporrea.org	26	27	42

Allende in Chile in 1973 as an explanatory framework when referring to current events in Venezuela, in particular the 2002 coup. In a sample of 21 news stories commemorating the defeat of 2002 broadcast in April 2010 on the pro-government networks Telesur and VTV, 16 mentioned or made reference at some point to the 1973 coup. The deconstruction of news provides a referent that can be used and understood by key leaders of public opinion, while putting the news story in a framework that has far more consensus among the public (as many accept that the Chilean coup was wrong) and therefore allow the message to reach a wider public beyond the hard-core constituencies of the Chavismo.

A Bad Memory of a Dirty War

Argentinean journalist Edi Zunino, in his book *Patria o Medios: la loca guerra de los Kirchner por el control de la realidad [Fatherland or Media: the crazy war of the Kirchners for the control of reality]* (2009), argues that the late President Nestor Kirchner and his wife Cristina Kirchner, who succeeded him as president of Argentina, made an orchestrated effort to re-write history regarding the dictatorship and the Dirty War that saw over 30,000 people disappear through the agency of the military rulers (2009, p. 28). Indeed, that is what appears to happen in the confrontation of the Kirchners with some of the most powerful and influential media conglomerates in Argentina; even though who is re-writing what is not entirely clear in this story.

To cut a long story short, President Kirchner ordered the authorities to review the sale of the country's main paper-manufacturing plant in the 1970s, arguing that it had happened under pressure from the military rulers. Kirchner's contention was that there was wrongdoing committed during the sale of Papel Prensa, which was sold by the Graiver family in 1976. In effect, Lidia Papaleo, widow of the then owner David Graiver who was killed in a mysterious air plane accident, was allegedly tortured and pushed to sell a stake in Papel Prensa to the newspapers *Clarin*, *La Nacion* and *La Razon* (Martinez, 2010); this despite the fact that the Clarin group and Isidoro Graiver (brother of David Graiver) maintain that these allegations were untrue; both parties maintained that the business was conducted legally (*La Nacion*, 2010). Isidoro Graiver went further to say that he was "surprised" to hear his brother's widow's allegations, as he himself had conducted the negotiations at the time. What derived from this was a very interesting and problematic exercise of interpreting and re-interpreting history, directly linked to whoever holds power in Argentina. As a media commentator wrote recently:

Argentina is fast approaching the 2011 presidential elections and the whole country is seized by the battle between the Kirchnerites and their fierce opposition. In this war, great names will be toppled and the ghosts of Argentina's past—specifically the lingering effects of the country's brutal military dictatorship—will certainly influence the country's future. (Mertnoff, 2011)

Indeed, the case of this story goes beyond the remit of the judiciary who would finally set the record straight, at least in terms of the law. It shows also how sensitive the whole issue is after so many years as it can still confer tangible power and influence to either side. The fact is that the characters of the story are so embedded in the narratives and histories that derived from the period in which the military junta ruled. These histories from the times of the dictatorships are re-emerging in the news because those holding office now come from the left of the political spectrum. One could argue that the Kirchners and their supporters are trying to use it as an opportunity to seize media power and widen their influence is a collateral matter. However, the point is that the Kirchners have already won, even if they never get the paper plant back to those who they think are its legitimate owners. This is because they, and those supporting them, have already created the necessary doubts among the readers of the three main newspapers and the other media outlets related to them with regards to the democratic credentials of the media group. They have effectively brought to the public's attention, after so many years, the role of these news media outlets during the dictatorship, reminding people that "somehow" these media groups participated in the Dirty War and supported the military junta. In so doing, they have managed to recover the memory of disappearance, torture and death, aligning it to the stories published and broadcast from now on in these media outlets, while undermining their legitimacy and that of their news stories and criticism against the government.

What the Kirchners have effectively done is to show the ideological status of the news media outlets opposing them, one that is clearly working to set a frame in which the Kirchners are seen as authoritarian (Romano, 2007). Therefore, even if the news media outlets opposing the government try to counter this by claiming that the Kirchners are only doing so to gain control of the media and limit freedom of speech, the Kirchnerites have already won the most important battle of framing the future news, because they have created a reference that links these media outlets to the most ruthless dictatorships in that country's history. Therefore, looking back to what they did and how they have handled this specific story, their actions now do not seem as irrational as they perhaps did at the start.

No Place for an Old Woman

The prospects of the new Brazilian president Dilma Rousseff in her dealings with the very powerful and influential Brazilian media are less promising than those of her predecessor, Luiz Inácio Lula da Silva. As a media commentator said during her swearing in as new president: "All the reasons that the right-wing media had to hate Lula are still there, plus she is a woman'.[2] In her case, the incorporation of history by the news media into their narratives and news items has been mainly used to frame the ability of Ms Rousseff to manage the eighth largest economy in the world. In the case of Brazil, the news media have always used a given interpretation of the past to contextualise the news in a certain manner. Ribeiro and Herschmann have pointed out that now, more than ever, the news media in Brazil show in their narratives a multiplicity of strategies that intersect the now and the past:

> The past is evoked to confirm the present. The media use of events of the past is not new. In the print media, for example, the mention and exaggerated uses of the past were common practice in newspapers of the 19th century. On the one hand, there is a historical dimension in journalism that is constantly used for symbolic (ideological) ends, which is constructed down the years by the journalists. (2008, p. 267)

These authors also argue that Brazilian media use the vestiges and facts from the past that arrive in the present to give a counterpoint to the permanent need of novelty in the contemporary world. The use of the past therefore is connected to a multiple textual typology and does not comprise a dimension visible only in the contemporary world. Moreover, in a world characterised by speed, immediacy and by a construction of the future that compresses the present—Paul Virilio called this "Dromology" (1977, p. 47)—the past acquires a singular significance. In this process of constructing ties between past, present and future, the news media, because of their role in the everyday life of people, have become fundamental in the consolidation of reality. When making visible to the audience/readers how a particular epoch lived its own temporality, the media through their narratives become the constructors of a particular historical dimension; since the construction of the meaning of time comes from their narratives (Ribeiro and Herschmann, 2008, p. 84). This is exactly the observation made by Mauro Malin in Observatorio da Imprensa—a left-wing organisation of journalists that works as a watchdog of the Brazilian press—when conmmenting on an article in the influential weekly magazine *Epoca* about Dilma's past as a "terrorist". Malin points out that the cover reportage of *Epoca* magazine (issue 639 of 14 August 2010) titled "O passado de Dilma" reduces 40 years of the public life of Dilma to the period of 1967–1979, when she participated in political organisations that adopted the armed struggle to oppose the dictators.

It is clear that those media outlets opposing Dilma tried to use an anti-communist frame, referred to as the fifth filter by Herman and Chomsky (1992 [1988]). Referring to the recently declassified documents of the Dirty War in Brazil, the magazine's cover page had the subtitle "unpublished documents disclose a history that she [Dilma] does not like to remember: her role in the armed struggle against the military regime". These documents referred to by the reporters of *Epoca* are the three legal processes against the Colina group (including Dilma) that add up to more than five million pages. The reporters "found" in these documents "evidence that Dilma dealt with guns, money, false documents, hidden places". However, as Malin points out in his critique: it would have been bizarre if she, having had a central role in the guerrilla organization, would have limited her participation to theoretical discussions, to washing dishes in the kitchen.

Indeed, Malin argues that the *Epoca* article ignores the amnesty decree from 31 years ago which pardoned key members of both sides and a series of subsequent events that wholly redeem and justify Dilma's use of violence in her youth. *Epoca*'s attempts to create doubts about her past by questioning Dilma's activities against the military dictatorship, which it says "are still without an answer". The article ends by asking if "Dilma has any regret concerning any of the attitudes and decisions taken at that time?" over 30 years ago but without really providing any context of how ruthless the dictatorship was. Malin answers *Epoca* by saying:

Put in this way, the response wouldn't even need to come from the candidate to the presidency of Brazilian Republic Dilma Rousseff. Anyone is capable of answering for her: yes. Life has no commitment with verisimilitude but it is implausible that Dilma does not admit to having made mistakes during that period. The question that the magazine insinuated is whether Dilma has a reflexive critique of her participation in the armed struggle. It would have been a good question. The armed struggle, daughter of despair and political isolation, facilitated the life of the hard line of the army and civil society. It made the revival of the democratic tradition more difficult.

In the *Epoca* reportage an indirect response from Dilma is quoted, which can have more than one interpretation: "I fought to help Brazil to change, and I ended up changing with Brazil". But, as Malin points out, even if we interpret this answer as a defence of the choice of the armed struggle, Dilma and all of her comrades from the guerrilla movement cannot be stigmatised. What Malin is suggesting is that historical judgements cannot be passed in a vacuum by selecting specific periods of one's history and then constructing from it an interpretation that favours one narrative. Indeed, *Epoca*'s article ignored the fact that the amnesty that pardoned Dilma over 30 years ago not only gave protection to those who, in the name of defending the 1964 military regime, committed crimes such as torture and killings, but also restored to all persecuted and punished by the dictatorial regime their rights as citizens, something which was ratified by the 1988 Constitution. Malin ends his column by saying that:

> If *Epoca* wants to re-discuss the Amnesty of 1979, in all its aspects, it needs to publish a wider and more in-depth reportage, which should start with the reasons and motivations that led to armed action prior to the emergence of Dilma's group, the military coup of 1964 and political and social consequences.

Indeed, the Brazilian media have recently become more aware of the importance of history in the framing of news stories and in defining the construction of news itself. When Adrianna Setemy, a doctoral student in history at the Federal University of Rio de Janeiro, went to the National Archives in Brasília in October, she was told that she could not have access to the records she normally uses to research the Foreign Ministry's role in the dictatorship-era fight against communism, because journalists had asked for them, and because the archives wanted to "protect the electoral process from the harm it could suffer from the information they contained" (Barnes, 2010). This anecdote perhaps is the best indicator that history indeed, in modern Brazil, is providing the scoop for some very inconvenient news stories and some selective details for the recitation of certain half-truths.

Conclusion

The celebrated Argentinean writer, journalist and former news editor Tomás Eloy Martínez wrote once that the language that journalists use is not only a matter of professional work, but overall an ethical strategy (Martínez, 1997). Martínez points out that this strategy allows the journalist to transcend the passive role of linking news and the public, permitting them to "think" reality by recognising emotions and hidden tensions within their surroundings. In bringing memories to the journalistic narratives, news sources and journalists highlight these emotions and tensions, therefore providing an understanding of the present. This is why, Martínez points out, journalists should not see themselves as "prosecutors, lawyers nor judges, but just witnesses" of the wider world.

In the cases studied here we have seen how the past is constructed so as to clarify the present, that is, as a kind of reservoir of singular and emblematic examples to be followed in the present. The use of history by journalists in the framing of their stories has the intention of providing the public with cumulative meaning, one that will define how audiences will read the news. This can explain why journalists in the region are now encouraged by their editors, media owners and government officials to include context; a task that has been made possible by the current state of polarised politics and facilitated by the access to historical archives and references provided by digital technologies such as the Internet.

It is not, however, a homogeneous exercise. While traditional power elites try to present ruptures and discontinuities, emerging actors, mainly left-wing politicians, are trying to bring back memory to show continuities. Leaders such as Evo Morales in Bolivia and even Daniel Ortega in Nicaragua, try to link their news media histories to that of the resistance and suffering of "their" people (indigenous, peasants, etc.), while rejecting altogether the notion of "progress" as framed in the West, which has been so important in substantiating the traditional and up to now predominant idea of "rupture". These divergent experiences also demand very distinctive approaches and practices when contextualising news stories in particular historical frameworks.

Despite these differences, there are some general trends to be observed in the region. For example, for the majority of left-wing political actors the recovery of memory is a crucial exercise, not only in justifying their right to hold power, but also in undermining that of their opponents. We can observe also that the news stories in these cases are made of narratives, which are distinct from those often articulated in European or US news media when reporting on Latin America as many journalists in Latin America adopt different practices from those of their peers in other parts of the world (Waisbord, 2000, p. xix).

For the local media studied here is not a New World, derived from a dreamed utopia, but a chance to grasp what almost could have happened; the tragic entelechy that tends to dominate the political imaginary in Latin America. In other words, this exercise of journalism has become in many cases a reflection of what has been referred to as the experiences of success and shortcomings of the left now in power in many places in Latin America (Weyland et al., 2010, p. 142). In this context, references to Salvador Allende in Chile and even Fidel Castro in Cuba (mostly in his ability to resist the United States after the end of the Cold War) are as valid as those of indigenous movements such as the Túpac Amaru rebellion, the failed project of the Great Colombia dreamt of by Bolívar.

In this sense, the past is responsible for clarifying the present and allowing a political understanding of it. But only in a way that serves those who manage to frame that reality to their own convenience. Indeed, memory is not demarcated in present and past but characterised by the convergence of multiple events that having happened in the past can still explain and justify present situations and legitimise current actions. This is what we see happening on one side of the spectrum. The de-constructing of reality that takes place in the media supporting the new left-wing regimes is performed as a substitute for traditional news gathering. In these exercises, journalists recover the past by highlighting its representations in our daily life, while selecting what is memorable and what is not. After all, as the late Federico Alvarez once said: "the media in Latin America have the power to forget and make us forget anything and anyone, only to rescue that memory when is convenient" (2010 [1978], p. 189).

Indeed, what the cases studied here suggest is that the dimension of forgetfulness and omission is also ideologically driven and therefore it has political implications for the articulation of meta-narratives. In the case of the recent debates surrounding media events in Latin America, the appropriation of history is used to create notional frames that define the understanding of the news stories in ways that confer power, through legitimacy, to some actors rather than others. In cases such as this, the use of history is reflected in the news story itself or in the selection of the articulating elements used in the narrative of that story, which often provide a completely different interpretation of the news presented in that same story.

Needless to say, at the core of this exercise is the matter of developing narratives that highlight either continuities or discontinuities, depending on what the elites controlling the media and political power want the public to remember or forget. The recent history of journalism in Latin America seems to be one of conveniently embedding selected memories and omissions into the stories that journalists tell to their audiences; an exercise that seems designed to help the new actors hold on to power for as long as they can.

NOTES

1. Interview with the authors on 12 January 2011.
2. Interview with Antonio Marcano, media analyst, on 16 December 2010.

REFERENCES

ALVAREZ, FEDERICO (2010 [1978]) *La Información Contemporánea*, Caracas: Agencia Venezolana de Noticias.

BARNES, TAYLOR (2010) "Dilma's Secrets", *Foreign Policy*, 30 December, http://www.foreignpolicy.com/articles/2010/12/30/dilmas_secrets_and_brazils?page=full, accessed January 2011.

BERGER, PETER and LUCKMANN, THOMAS (1975 [1966]) *The Social Construction of Reality*, London: Penguin.

DÍAZ RANGEL, ELEAZAR (1991) *La Información Internacional en América Latina*, Caracas: Monte Avila Editores.

FAUNDES, JUAN JORGE (1998) "Una perspectiva estratégica y compleja del periodismo latinoamericano", *Diálogos de Comunicación* 51, pp. 25–36.

FERREIRA, LEONARDO (2006) *Centuries of Silence: the story of Latin American journalism*, New York: Praeger.

FITZGERALD, TIMOTHY (2007) *Discourses of Civility and Barbarity*, Cambridge: Cambridge University Press.

FORD, ANÍBAL (1999) *La Marca de la Bestia: identificación, desigualdades e infoentretenimiento en la sociedad contemporánea*, Buenos Aires: Norma.

HERMAN, EDWARD and CHOMSKY, NOAM (1992 [1988]) *Manufacturing Consent: the political economy of the mass media*, New York: Pantheon.

KITSCHELT, HERBERT, HAWKINS, KIRK, LUNA, JUAN PABLO, ROSAS, GILLERMO and ZECHMEISTER, ELITABETH (2010) *Latin American Party Systems*, Cambridge: Cambridge University Press.

LA NACION (2010) "Isidoro Graiver refuta a la Presidenta", 25 August, http://www.lanacion.com.ar/nota.asp?nota_id=1297876, accessed January 2011.

LAKOFF, GEORGE (2004) *Don't Think of an Elephant*, White River Junction, VT: Chelsea Green Publishing.

LAKOFF, GEORGE (2008) *The Political Mind: why you can't understand 21st-century American politics with an 18th-century brain*, New York: Viking Adult Press.

LORETI, DAMIAN (2005) *América Latina y la Libertad de Expression*, Buenos Aires: Grupo Editorial Norma.

LUGO, JAIRO (2008) *The Media in Latin America*, Maidenhead: Open University Press.

LUGO, JAIRO and CAÑIZÁLEZ, ANDRES (2007) "Telesur: estrategia geopolítica con fines integracionistas", *Revista ConFines* 1(6), pp. 53–64.

LUGO, JAIRO and ROMERO, JUAN (2003) "From Friends to Foes: Venezuela's media goes from consensual space to confrontational actor", *Revista Sincronía* 4(2), http://sincronia.cucsh.udg.mx/lugoromeroinv02.htm, accessed November 2010.

MARTIN BARBERO, JESUS (1996) *De los Medios a las Mediaciones: comunicación, cultura y hegemonía*, Barcelona: Editorial Gustavo Gili.

MARTINEZ, NICOLE (2010) "President Kirchner Delivers Speech Concerning Papel Prensa Controversy", *The Argentina Independent*, 25August, http://www.argentinaindependent.com/currentaffairs/newsroundups/roundupsargentina/president-kirchner-delivers-speech-concerning-papel-prensa-controversy-/, accessed December 2010.

MARTÍNEZ, TOMÁS ELOY (1997) *Periodismo y Narración: desafíos para el siglo XXI*, Asamblea de la Sociedad Interamericana de Prensa, 26 October, http://local.fnpi.org:8990/download/periodismo.pdf, accessed 23 November 2010.

MERTNOFF, AZUL (2010) "Hot Times in Argentina Leading to the 2011 Presidential Election", *The Cutting Edge*, 20 September, http://www.thecuttingedgenews.com/index.php?article = 12551&pageid=&pagename=, accessed January 2011.

MUJICA, HECTOR (2010 [1967]) *El imperio de la noticia. Algunos problemas de la informacio'n en el mundo contemporáneo*, Caracas: Agencia Venezolana de Noticias.

PION-BERLIN, DAVID (Ed.) (2001) *Civil–Military Relations in Latin America: new analytical perspectives*, Chapel Hill: The University of North Carolina Press.

RAMOS, REINALDO (1991) "Tardaremos décadas en salir de la crisis de la deuda externa", *Diario Panorama*, 21 May, p. A15.

RIBEIRO, ANA PAULA GOULART and HERSCHMANN, MICAEL (2008) *Communicacao e Historia: interfaces e novas abordagens*, Rio de Janeiro: Globo Universidade.

ROMANO, MARÍA BELÉN (2007) "Kirchner y el ejercicio de su poder: representaciones en la prensa escrita", *Universidad Nacional de Tucumán*, http://www.fhuc.unl.edu.ar/sal/ejes_tematicos/analisis_del_discurso/romano.pdf, accessed January 2011.

SCHLESINGER, PHILIP (1978) *Putting "Reality"*, Together, London: Constable.

SOLEY, LAWRENCE (1992) *The News Shapers: the sources who explain the news*, New York: Praeger Publishers.

TUCHMAN, GAYE (1972) "Objectivity as a Strategic Ritual", *American Journal of Sociology* 77, pp. 660–79.

WAISBORD, SILVIO (2000) *Watchdog Journalism in South America: news, accountability and democracy*, New York: Columbia University Press.

WEYLAND, KURT, MADRID, RAUL and HUNTER, WENDY (2010) *Leftist Governments in Latin America: successes and shortcomings*, Cambridge: Cambridge University Press.

VIRILIO, PAUL (1977) *Speed and Politics: an essay on dromology*, New York: Semiotext.

ZUNINO, EDI (2009) *Patria o Medios: la loca guerra de los Kirchner por el control de la realidad*, Buenos Aires: Sudamericana.

Index

Page numbers in *Italics* represent tables.
Page numbers followed by a represent appendix.
Page numbers followed by n represent endnotes.

INDEX

www.routledge.com/9780415622851

Related titles from Routledge

Explorations in Global Media Ethics

Edited by Muhammad Ayish and Shakuntala Rao

Studies of global media and journalism have repeatedly returned to discussions of ethics. This book highlights the difficulty that journalists encounter when establishing appropriate ethical practices and marks the pressing importance of global media ethics as a subject of current debate. A wide range of contributors – both scholars and practitioners of journalism – identify how changes in journalism practice, developments in new media technologies, legal regulations, and shifting patterns of ownership all play a role in creating ethical tensions for journalists, with some chapters in the book suggesting practical solutions to this pertinent issue. The growing need to faithfully represent other diverse cultural groups is also considered.

Explorations in Global Media Ethics recognises that, with the escalation of globalisation and a public striving for honest quality media, journalists around the world face an increasing pressure to comply with and simultaneously satisfy diverse ethical practices at both a local and a global level. The book sympathises with the position of the journalist and calls for greater consideration of his ambiguous role.

This book was originally published as a special issue of *Journalism Studies*.

May 2012: 246 x 174: 124 pp
Hb: 978-0-415-62285-1
£85 / $135

For more information and to order a copy visit
www.routledge.com/9780415622851

Available from all good bookshops

www.routledge.com/9780415622899

Related titles from Routledge

Foreign Correspondence

Edited by Maxwell John Hamilton and Regina G. Lawrence

Despite the importance of foreign news, its history, transformation and indeed its future have not been much studied. The need to redress this neglect and the desire to assess the impact of new media technologies on the future of journalism, including foreign correspondence, provide the motivation for this stimulating, exciting and thought-provoking book.

While the old economic models supporting news have crumbled in the wake of new media technologies, these changes have the potential to bring new and improved ways to inform people of foreign news. Journalism is being transformed by the effortlessly quick sharing of information across national boundaries. As such, we need to reconsider foreign correspondence and explore where such reporting is headed. This book discusses the current state and future prospects for foreign correspondence across the full range of media platforms, and assesses developments in the reporting of overseas news for audiences, governments and foreign policy in both contemporary and historical settings around the globe.

This book was originally published as a special issue of *Journalism Studies*.

May 2012: 246 x174: 160 pp
Hb: 978-0-415-62289-9
£85 / $135

For more information and to order a copy visit
www.routledge.com/9780415622899

Available from all good bookshops

JOURNALISM PRACTICE

Volume 5 Number 6 December 2011

JOURNALISM PRACTICE

Routledge
Taylor & Francis Group
ISSN: 1751-2786

Editor: **Bob Franklin,** *Cardiff University, UK*

Journalism Practice provides opportunities for reflective, critical and research-based studies focused on the professional practice of journalism. *Journalism Practice*'s primary concern is to analyse and explore issues of practice and professional relevance. The journal aims to complement current trends to expansion in the teaching and analysis of journalism practice within the academy, reflection on the emergence of a reflective curriculum and thereby help to consolidate journalism as an intellectual discipline within the landscape of higher education.

Journalism Practice is devoted to: the study and analysis of significant issues arising from journalism as a field of professional practice; relevant developments in journalism training and education, as well as the construction of a reflective curriculum for journalism; analysis of journalism practice across the distinctive but converging media platforms of magazines, newspapers, online, radio and television; and the provision of a public space for practice-led, scholarly contributions from journalists as well as academics.

www.tandfonline.com/rjop

Routledge
Taylor & Francis Group

0 1341 1485786 2